Defending the Majesty of Islam
Indonesia's Front Pembela Islam, 1998–2003

T0324295

DEFENDING THE MAJESTY OF ISLAM
INDONESIA'S FRONT PEMBELA ISLAM 1998–2003

JAJANG JAHRONI

ASIAN MUSLIM ACTION NETWORK

SILKWORM BOOKS

This publication is partially funded by The Rockefeller Foundation.

ISBN–10: 974-9511-11-5
ISBN–13: 978-974-9511-11-4

First published in 2008 by

Silkworm Books
6 Sukkasem Road, T. Suthep, Chiang Mai 50200, Thailand
E-mail address: info@silkwormbooks.com
Website: http://www.silkwormbooks.com

We acknowledge Bonnie Brereton for her editorial assistance.

Typeset by Silk Type in Warnock Pro 10 pt.
Printed in Thailand by O. S. Printing House, Bangkok

5 4 3 2 1

FOREWORD

Problematizing views from within "Islam(s)" in Southeast Asia

In 1953 the late Gustav von Grunebaum organized a conference of leading European scholars of Islam, the first to undertake a historical and critical self-understanding of "Islamic studies." The conference examined relationships among Muslims, and between Islam and various cultures. It found that the assumptions and methods used in fields of study like Islamic history lagged a century behind those used in European history. One year later Bernard Lewis remarked that the history of the Arabs had been written primarily in Europe by historians with no knowledge of Arabic and Arabists with no knowledge of history.[1]

Half a century later, research on the subject has changed. There is an increasing number of studies on Islam written by Muslims who know the faith, the cultures, and the practices in different contexts—the works by Akbar Ahmad, Mahmoud Mumdani, Chandra Muzaffar, and Nurcholish Madjid are just a few examples among many. Also changed is the global context itself. Now perhaps more than ever, "Islam" is more than just a description of a fifteen-century-old faith shared by one-and-a-half billion people. The word has strong emotive qualities for those both within and outside the faith. Two decades ago the late Edward Said wrote, "For the right, Islam represents barbarism; for the left, medieval theocracy; for the center, a kind of distasteful exoticism. In all camps, however, there is agreement that even though little enough is known about the Islamic world there is not much to be approved of there."[2] It is therefore important to understand, from their own perspectives, the contemporary problems that Muslims are facing.

Works in this series, Islam in Southeast Asia: Views from Within, join many other writings on Islam by authors at the periphery of scholarship,

v

using assumptions and methods that may no longer differ from those used in the centers of learning. But if such is the case, how is this series different from the other writings on Islam that are presently flooding the popular and academic landscapes?

To state the obvious, this series addresses Islam in Southeast Asia. In relation to the Islamic world, where the sacred geography, history, and language of the Middle East seems to have established that region as the center, Southeast Asia is clearly seen as the periphery. But it is misleading to conceptualize Southeast Asia as a single sociocultural entity. As is true elsewhere in the world, societies in Southeast Asia are heterogeneous. Muslims in Indonesia and Malaysia, for example, lead lives that differ from those in Thailand and the Philippines because of the different realities facing majority and minority populations in the respective countries. Furthermore, whether Muslims constitute a minority or a majority, their lives differ again when seen in contexts influenced by Javanese culture, British colonialism, Filipino Catholicism, or Theravada Buddhism, among other things. In short, the cultural topography of Southeast Asia is a rich multiplicity.

Consequently, Islam as believed in and practiced by people in the diverse worlds of Southeast Asia is not necessarily singular, since there could be as many Islams as the various contexts that constitute them.[3] The problems facing Muslims in Southeast Asia will therefore vary. Those portrayed by researchers in this series are unusual, and their analysis is at times groundbreaking, but what they underscore is that Southeast Asian Muslims struggle with multiple identities in sociocultural contexts destabilized by globalizing forces. In addition, the fact that this research is carried out by young Muslim scholars is important; the "new generation" factor could explain both the distinctive set of problems these researchers are interested in and the fresh approaches they use.

The "views from within" approach, however, is not without its own potential problems. To engage in studies claiming to be "views from within" is in some ways to guard against the study of "others" as the study of one's own self, because in such a situation writers face other types of realities that are possibly distorted in some other ways. It is therefore important for readers to appreciate the effort researchers make to situate themselves at a distance that gives them a better perspective on the social realities of their subject while retaining their sensitivity towards, and ability to relate to, the people they are studying.[4]

At a time when Islamophobia is on the rise,[5] it is essential to find fresh perspectives that will allow us to understand the new problems and tensions facing Muslims in contemporary Southeast Asian societies, and to articulate the ways in which they negotiate their lives as members of communities of faith in a fast-changing world. This series of studies by young Muslim scholars of Southeast Asia is an important step in this direction.

Chaiwat Satha-Anand
Faculty of Political Science
Thammasat University, Bangkok

Notes

1. Azim Nanji, ed, *Mapping Islamic Studies: Genealogy, Continuity and Change* (Berlin and New York: Mouton de Gruyter, 1997), xii.

2. Edward Said, *Covering Islam* (New York: Pantheon, 1981), xv.

3. Aziz Al-Azmeh, *Islams and Modernities* (London and New York: Verso, 1996).

4. I have discussed the problem of alterity in conducting research on Muslim studies in Chaiwat Satha-Anand, *The Life to this World: Negotiated Muslim Lives in Thai Society* (Singapore and New York: Marshall Cavendish, 2005), 25–26.

5. Akbar S. Ahmad, *Islam under Siege: Living Dangerously in a Post-Honor World* (Cambridge: Polity Press, 2004), 36–39.

CONTENTS

The *kyai kampung* (village religious scholars) are *ulama* and *kyai* (preachers) who are unknown to most people. They give religious teachings, from one mosque to another, from one village to another. Their insights are as sharp as knives and swords. Watch out when they get angry. They are angry because of Allah, not because of their low desires. Their hearts are beating. The hearts of their students and followers are also beating, waiting for the command of *jihad*, which can happen at any time. If the drums of war have been beaten by those consistent *ulama*, if the commands of *jihad* have been announced by the *kyai* of the Hereafter, the Muslim people would come like a flock of birds, welcoming the *jihad* and waiting for His forgiveness. They are the soldiers of Allah, who are ready to meet death with smiles and happiness. "Live with dignity or die as a *syuhada* (martyr)."

—Habib Muhammad Rizieq Syihab
Imam Besar (Chief Leader) of the FPI

INTRODUCTION

Indonesia's 1998 Reformasi brought with it the long overdue freedom of expression, including the opportunity for Islamic fundamentalist groups to assert themselves as never before.[1] In addition, the movement spawned a number of new organizations whose aim is to either establish an Islamic state or apply Islamic law. The emergence of these organizations is closely related to the spirit of the reformation, and now nearly every day one can see people gathering in Senayan Jakarta, where the House of Representatives office is located, to express their aspirations to the members of Parliament.

Gatherings like this were few and far between in the Suharto era,[2] beginning in the late 1960s, when Indonesians did not have the opportunity to express their opinions. Suharto applied what is often called the de-ideologization of all social and political power. Politics was cleansed of any religious embellishment and Pancasila was imposed as the sole ideology to be adopted by all political and social organizations in the country.[3]

Islamic fundamentalism, as manifested in the activities of several radical groups now flourishing in Indonesia's open political climate, refers to a movement that aims to revive the Golden Age of Islam.[4] In this view, a return to the Qur'an and the Sunnah, or the example of the Prophet Muhammad, is the only avenue available for Muslims to achieve dignity in this mortal life. The lives of the Prophet and his Companions are regarded as ideal models to be imitated by Muslims. Fundamentalism calls for the renewal of the confession of faith (*shahada*) of the Muslim community, which it contends, has long been contaminated by secular ideas that are incompatible with Islam. The unity of the Muslim community (*ummah*), which is based on the principle of *tauhid* (the unity of God), should be reestablished to prevent Muslims from losing their commitment to Islam. Fundamentalists believe that as long as Muslims are not strongly committed to Islam, and as long as their hearts are impure, they will be punished

1

by God. Muslim countries' lack of development, dependence on Western aid, and loss of dignity are believed to be God's acts of punishment. Fundamentalists believe that if Muslims accept Islam unconditionally, they will once again regain their dignity and live in this world with respect.

On the one hand, the development of Islamic fundamentalism in Indonesia has been influenced to some degree by Suharto's strategy of marginalizing Muslims in social and political life. The mushrooming of Islamic fundamentalism between 1999 and 2003 is like the eruption of a volcano following decades of repression under the Suharto regime. On the other hand, this development is inseparable from the global influence of Islamic resurgence over the last quarter of the past century. At the same time, the modernization and globalization pervading all parts of the world have also brought major changes into Muslims' lives. These sociological factors are all interwoven in the rise of Islamic fundamentalism in Indonesia.

The present study explores the roots of Islamic fundamentalism in Indonesia with particular focus on one movement, Front Pembela Islam (FPI). It begins by examining the interplay of several factors that set the stage for the emergence of various indigenous fundamentalist movements. These factors include the status of Muslims under the Suharto regime, modernization, global Islamic movements, and the growth of an educated urban population. The study then relates the biography of Habib Muhammad Rizieq Syihab, who is a witness to the changing face of Jakarta as well as a founding father of FPI and its current head. After discussing the group's creation and paramilitary activities, it examines FPI's ideology with particular reference to the goal of establishing Islamic law in Indonesia. Finally, it analyzes FPI's organizational and social bases, recruitment practices, and training methods, including the use of religious teachings to justify the deliberate destruction of entertainment places that are the site of activities such as gambling, prostitution, and drinking, which Islamic teaching considers to be corrupting (*kemungkaran*).

STATUS OF MUSLIMS DURING THE
NEW ORDER (1967–1998)

During the first two decades of Suharto's New Order administration (which lasted from 1967 to 1998), Muslims were virtually absent in significant administrative positions in the country. Instead of appointing Muslims to his government, Suharto invited the Christian and Chinese minority groups who were dependent on him to become his political partners. This decision is related to his belief that Muslims would be a political threat to his power. It is obvious that Suharto wanted his position to become solidly entrenched before inviting any other group to share power. Fully backed by the armed forces and his political machine, the Golkar Party, Suharto ruled the country for about thirty-two years with absolute power.[5]

Indonesia was in a deep economic crisis just before Suharto came to power, following the 1965 bloody coup d'état. One of his first measures early in his presidency was to invite economists such as Widjojo Nitisastro to serve on his board of economic advisors. Later called the "Berkeley mafia,"[6] this board was charged with overcoming the crisis, stabilizing the *rupiah*, slowing down inflation, and making long-term strategic economic plans. The results were incredible. In a short time, Suharto was able to solve major economic problems and make significant improvements, and over the following years, economic growth stabilized, averaging 7 percent per year.[7]

The short-term strategies undertaken by the Berkeley mafia during the New Order economy were extremely successful. But implementing the long-term strategy of the so-called trickle-down effect was a disaster, and the 1997 economic crisis was in some part related to earlier mistakes in strategic planning. The strategy had been set up for big business enterprises. Its working theory was based on the assumption that development projects in industry, agriculture, trade, banking, finance, export-import, construction, information, transportation, telecommunication, mines,

3

and tourism would be followed by a trickle-down effect to all segments of society. But what actually happened was totally different.

By the 1980s, as a result of this strategy a number of tycoons, predominantly Chinese and Christian, controlled large segments of the national economy. The money, instead of trickling down to a broad base of Indonesian communities, collected around the tycoons' families. A common scenario was one in which a single company belonging to a particular person expanded to other sectors controlled by that person's cronies. Rather than providing credit, loans, or grants, the strategy produced fertile ground for corruption, collusion, and nepotism.[8]

The majority of Muslims did not have any significant role in these national business activities. They became the excluded groups. What they were able to do was largely limited to medium and small businesses and mainly in the informal sectors. This reality was seen as unfair by most Muslims and it increased resistance against the Chinese at both the grassroots and middle-class levels. As the gap between the wealthy Chinese and the working-class ethnic Indonesians became wider, resistance grew stronger. Paralleling this resistance was a growing resentment against the Christians, Golkar, Indonesia's armed forces (ABRI), and Suharto's family.[9]

By the late 1980s, however, Suharto's approach to Islam changed significantly due to several factors, including increasing tensions with the minority groups. It was reported that he became angry when the notorious L. B. Murdani, a Catholic and the commander of the Indonesian armed forces, questioned him about his family's pervasive business ownership.[10] Soon afterwards, Murdani was dismissed from his post and replaced by Faisal Tanjung, a conservative Muslim and Murdani opponent. After this event, Suharto's relationship with the minorities deteriorated further, while those with Muslims began to improve.

It is likely that Suharto began to realize that genuine legitimacy had to come from the majority. During the last decade of his term, he approached Muslims and shifted to what is sometimes called "conservative Islamism."[11]

This shift was also related to the phenomenon of Islamic resurgence taking place in the country. The resurgence was partly the result of the national education project initiated during the first years of his term. Islam was seen as too powerful and too important to be abandoned. In those years, a set of policies and programs was established, including the Islamic banking system, the Muslim intellectual association, the application of Islamic law in limited form, permission for Muslim women to wear the *jilbab* (women's veil) in the public schools, permission for the publication of Islamic magazines, and allowing Islamic religious programs to be broadcast on television.

Following these policies, Suharto returned to practicing Islam. In 1991, after having long been acknowledged as a strong adherent of Javanese mysticism, Suharto, together with his family, performed *hajj*, the pilgrimage to Mecca, and added "Muhammad" to his name. Some Muslim leaders welcomed these changes, believing that they indicated a real shift in Suharto's approach to Islam and that he wanted to assure his Muslim fellows that he had really changed for the better. But others reacted to these changes with cynicism, saying that they were too little, too late. They urged Muslims not to be manipulated further by Suharto and argued that all these acts were merely designed to strengthen his power base.

ISLAMIC MOVEMENTS IN THE 1980s

In Indonesia there are numerous groups claiming to represent the aspirations of the Muslim majority. One group that Robert Hefner has termed "regimist Muslims" consists of the bureaucrats, technocrats, and intellectuals who are strongly attached to conservative Islam.[12] At the grassroots level the majority of Muslims are not engaged with this group. Another is the Indonesian Muslim Intellectuals Association (ICMI), the largest conservative Islamist project, which did have some impact on the life of Indonesian Muslims. However, a great number of Muslims are still attached to the established religious organizations such as the Nahdatul Ulama (NU) and Muhammadiyah.[13]

In addition, in the late 1970s and early 1980s, a number of campus-based Muslim organizations were founded. There are at least two main groups to be noted here. The first was influenced by the ideas of the Muslim Brotherhood of Egypt, while the second showed strong Shiite tendencies; in practice, however, there were no obvious distinctions between the two groups. Both had vague schemes that were a combination of various ideas. They were not really concerned with the ideological boundaries between the schools of Islamic thought, for they claimed it was not in keeping with the spirit of Islam.

Preferring to keep a low profile, they had no formal organizational structure. They referred to themselves in different ways, sometimes as *usroh* (family) *harakah* (movement), and sometimes as *ikhwan* and *akhwat* (brothers and sisters).[14] Names did not seem to be very important. These organizations were supported by a large number of students and were responsible for the initiation of the Islamization movement on various campuses.

Apparently much support for these movements came from the growing aspirations of young Muslim students who favored Islamic sociopolitical ideas. This emerging approach to understanding Islam in a modern and holistic manner (*kaaffah*) held that the established Muslim organizations such as the NU and Muhammadiyah were "half-hearted" or "not serious" in realizing the ideals of Islam, and that their innovations (*bid'ah*), in fact, reduced the Islamic spirit.

Meanwhile, student organizations such as the Muslim Students' Association (HMI), Muhammadiyah Students' Association (IMM), and Indonesian Muslim Students' Movement (PMII, an NU-linked student organization), were busily engaged in developing intellectual discourses.

In the early 1980s, a new spirit of activism began to pervade several campuses. An increasing number of *jilbab* and *burqa* (women's cloaks) were seen among the female students, replacing the previously popular mini skirts, jeans, and T-shirts. At the same time, many male students grew long beards and wore the *koko* (traditional Indonesian shirt). Keeping a low profile in public, they created small circles for discussion (*halaqah*) where various Islamic topics were addressed. It was not uncommon for discussions to be held door-to-door, informally.[15]

These movements were marked by various attempts to seek an alternative Islam that was capable of realizing its ideals.[16] This alternative Islam was sought as a substitute for existing Islam, which was considered impotent. The new Islam was expected to be able to realize an *ummah* (Muslim community) as the ideal form of community. To create such a community, the movement's discourse started with the meaning of *shahada*, or declaration of faith. While *shahada* is usually understood as the formal utterance of several words indicating that one embraces Islam, these groups interpret it in a very sophisticated way.[17] To them, Islam is understood as a holistic system, a way of life, and an ideology by which Muslims can achieve their ultimate goals. Islam is not only concerned with personal affairs and an individual's commitment to Islam, but also with social, economic, cultural, and political issues.

This alternative Islam holds that if Muslims understood the meaning of *shahada* correctly, they would be able to understand other religious

7

concepts, such as Islamic moral conduct (*akhlaq*) and the purpose of religious devotion (*ibadah*), without any difficulty. They would also practice all religious obligations without hesitation. Thus, the new activists were concerned with creating a new system to replace the system of ignorance (*jahiliyah*) and infidelity (*kekufuran*). They criticized the established Islamic organizations for misunderstanding fundamental religious principles, the result of which was that although Muslims comprised the majority of the Indonesian population, most of them did not practice their religion wholeheartedly.

Islamic movements of the 1970s and 1980s were fully backed by young Muslim intellectuals standing hand-in-hand with university students as well as middle-class Muslim families. Most of these intellectuals were graduates of Western universities; only a few were from Middle Eastern institutions. During that period it appears that public perception of Islam and Muslims gradually became more positive. Islam came to be seen as an elegant and modern religion. Growing numbers of people joined Islamic organizations, the veil and *burqa* grew in popularity, discussions on Islam were held in many places, and increasing numbers of people made the pilgrimage to Mecca.

GLOBAL INFLUENCES ON THE ISLAMIC MOVEMENT

The Islamic movement in Indonesian was also encouraged by a number of events taking place in the Muslim world, such as the 1979 Islamic revolution. Although Indonesian Muslims do not subscribe to Shiite Islam, this remarkable event inspired their movements and once again assured them that Islam was in fact able to serve as an ideology of resistance. Shiism has become an important issue in the country since then, raising both positive and negative opinions within Muslim communities. Eventually, because of certain intellectual figures, the perception of Shiism gradually changed. It should be acknowledged that Shiism contributed to the development of Islamic discourses in Indonesia.[18]

A number of works by modern Iranian thinkers such as the Ayatollah Ruhollah Khomeini, Ali Shariati, and Murtadha Mutahhari enjoyed greater readership and influenced the ideological formulation of Indonesian Islamic movements. Some publishing houses in the country specialized in circulating Shiite books, while others focused on the Islamic movement in general. It is amazing that these books were always sold out. The publication of Islamic books seems to have reached its peak in the 1990s, when Islamic publishing houses dominated the entire exhibition hall at every book fair in the country. Certain titles were reprinted numerous times.

Balancing the Shiite point of view were Sunni ideas, including those of Sayyid Qutb, Hasan al-Banna, Said Hawa, and Yusuf Qardhawi. The relationship between Indonesian Muslims and Middle East thinkers had existed long before their contact with Iranian Shiite thought.[19] Indonesia has regularly sent students to study at al-Azhar University in Cairo, Egypt. Some of them made contacts with the Muslim Brotherhood while there and brought home its ideas. Syed Qutb's Qur'anic commentary, *Fi Dhilal al-Quran* (In the Shade of the Qur'an), soon become very popular in Indonesia. To a lesser degree, contacts were also established with

Islamic movements in India and Pakistan, leading to the dissemination of the ideas of Maulana Abul Ala Maududi and Maulana Hasan al-Nadwi.

THE THREAT OF MODERNIZATION

The modernization process in Muslim countries that became independent from Western colonialism failed to spread uniformly during the last quarter of the twentieth century. The main reason for this failure is that most of these countries were still functioning in traditional or transitional modes. Manuel Castells points out that the social roots of Islamic fundamentalism emerged as "a reaction to the failure of economic modernization in most Muslim countries in the 1970s and 80s."[20] As a result, many aspects of life changed drastically, bringing serious social problems and dislocations.

The problem became more complicated as modernization also brought with it trends of rationalization and secularization. Islam does not accommodate secularism, which represents the dark side of modernism, thereby making Muslims confused about whether to accept modernization in toto or in part. In a similar vein, Muslims are generally suspicious of new ideas imported from the West, such as democracy, gender equality, and human rights. With respect to these ideas, Muslims do not have a single, unified response but react in various ways ranging from total rejection to total acceptance.

In the Indonesian context, modernization was affecting the majority and minority sections of the population in significantly different ways. The Indonesian Muslims were the least prepared to come to terms with modernity. From the 1970s onwards, the minority groups comprising only 12 percent of the population started to enjoy a high-tech lifestyle and build modern business enterprises; at the same time, the Muslims, who comprise the majority or 88 percent, were still struggling with poverty and illiteracy. Only a few Muslim groups from middle-class families had relatively better living conditions than before; the majority lived under very poor conditions.

Moreover, in the late 1970s and 1980s, the country witnessed great waves of urbanization. Thousands of people, both men and women, most of them traditional peasants, were expelled from their villages after their lands were sold at very low prices to wealthy people from big cities. They migrated to urban areas looking for a better life, but were unable to compete with their fellow Indonesians from the minority groups. Their frustration, fear, and anger at this unexpected outcome of their movement to the cities grew rapidly. The uneducated and unskilled urbanites began to form religious discussion circles that were soon transformed into ideologized resistance groups protesting against injustice and corruption. Castells explains the situation succinctly.

> Thus, a young, urban population, with a high level of education as a result of the first wave of modernization, was frustrated in its expectations, as the economy faltered and new forms of cultural dependency settled in. It was joined in its discontent by impoverished masses expelled from rural areas to cities by the unbalanced modernization of agriculture. This social mixture was made explosive by the crisis of the nation-state, whose employees, including military personnel, suffered declining living standards, and lost faith in the nationalist project.[21]

This setting provided the context for the evolution of a new type of activist leader, well versed in Islamic teaching and at the same time endowed with the capacity to interpret Islamic teachings in radical new ways.

BIOGRAPHY OF HABIB MUHAMMAD RIZIEQ SYIHAB

Habib Muhammad Rizieq Syihab, who was to emerge as the leader of one of Indonesia's most prominent radical Islamic groups, Front Pembela Islam (FPI), was born in Jakarta on August 24, 1965 in an *ahl al-bait* (descendants of the Prophet Muhammad) family. The title *habib* (pl. *habaib*) indicates this social status. His father, Husein, was an activist. In 1937, together with colleagues and friends, Husein established the Indonesian Arab Boy Scouts (PAI), which later changed into the Indonesian Islam Boy Scouts (PII). He led the organization from 1930 to 1945. He was later involved in spying for the Indonesian forces and in 1945 was arrested by the Dutch and sentenced to death, but avoided the sentence through the help of a native person working for the Dutch.

After Indonesia's independence in 1945, Husein, like most other members of *habaib* families, worked as a religious teacher and had a close relationship with Habib Ali ibn Abdurrahman a-Habsyi, one of the most respected *habib* during that time. He founded an Islamic learning center in Kwitang Jakarta and had a great following among both the Hadhrami[22] and Betawinese communities. Husein died in 1966, one year after the birth of his son Rizieq. Rizieq never met his father. His mother, Syarifah Sidah Al-Attas, who like his father was from an *ahl al-bait* family, took over responsibility for his education.

Rizieq obtained a relatively secular education, going to elementary school in Petamburan and to secondary school in Pejompongan. Because of security reasons, he was moved, somewhat surprisingly, to Bethel Secondary School, a Christian institution located not far from his house. He is said to have rejected this move initially, as he was worried about being influenced by ideas contradictory to his faith. After some assurance by his mother, however, he accepted it and spent several years there. In this Christian environment he was reportedly very critical of his teachers, especially on religious matters. It is reported that in school he once spoke on the Islamic view of Jesus Christ, which holds that he is not divine but merely one of Allah's prophets.

After completing high school, Rizieq wanted to study in the Middle East. Lacking knowledge of Arabic, he enrolled in the Institute for the Study of Islam and Arabic (LIPIA) in Jakarta, which was financially backed by the Saudi Arabian government. Subsequently he went to study in the faculty of law at King Saud University in Riyadh, Saudi Arabia. It is important to note that the Saudi government donated a million dollars annually, channeled through LIPIA or the Organization of Islamic Countries (OIC), to recruit young Muslims to study in Saudi Arabia. Before heading to Saudi Arabia, Rizieq married Syarifah Fadlun, the granddaughter of the well-known *mufti* of Batavia, Sayyid Uthman ibn Abdullah ibn Yahya.[23]

During his studies in Saudi Arabia, Rizieq, like most Indonesian students, served as a guide to pilgrims during the *hajj* season and also worked for the Indonesian embassy in Riyadh. After graduating in 1990, he spent a year as a teaching assistant in a Riyadh high school. In 1992 he returned to Indonesia and spent the next year as an active preacher giving religious talks to the community. Interested in furthering his studies, he then enrolled in the International Islamic University Malaysia, but feeling that his community needed him, he quit after a semester and returned to Indonesia to become a preacher once again.[24]

Like most Hadhrami communities, the one in Betawi presented itself symbolically as both Islamic and Arab. The people maintained the traditional clothing styles of their predecessors in the eighteenth and nineteenth centuries, used their family names, and spoke in Arabic to maintain their distinct identity. They also established an organization called Jami'at al-Khair (community of righteousness) as an educational institution offering courses in Arabic studies, such as the geography of the Middle East.[25] With the spread of modernization in Indonesia, some Hadhrami adopted new cultural practices, such as allowing the women to marry ordinary non-Sayyid men. This change eventually caused a conflict between the various Hadhrami groups.[26]

Based on their religious adherence, the Hadhrami of Indonesia can be divided into three groups. The first group, the puritans, consists of Hadhrami who are strongly committed to Islam as a pristine religion. Their roots are found in the teachings of Sayyid Uthman, who considered *tarekat*/Sufism a deviation from Islam.[27] The second group, the moderates, is composed of those Hadhrami who adapted to religious practices like those of the moderate Nahdatul Ulama, the largest Muslim organization in Indonesia. This group is represented by Sayyid Aqil Husein al-Munawwar, the current minister of religious affairs, who is also a member of the Nahdatul Ulama. The third group, secular Muslims, consists of the Hadhrami who enjoyed privileges during the era of Dutch colonialism and were educated in the Dutch education system. It is represented by the former foreign minister of Indonesia, Ali Alatas, and by Ahmad Albar, an Indonesian music celebrity. The secular Hadhrami are not very attached to religion. Like their parents and grandparents, they usually send their children to secular educational institutions.

Habib Muhammad Rizieq Syihab comes from the puritan group, although he spent some years in secular schools. Most puritans send their children to religious schools or *madrasah* built by their fellow Hadhrami. Many of them have studied in various *pesantren* (Islamic boarding schools) in East Java, especially Malang, where there is a strong Hadhrami settlement. During the colonial period, they went to Hadhramaut for higher religious education given by various *shakh* and *ulama*. In post-independence Indonesia, this tradition has been abandoned, since younger Hadhrami, unlike their predecessors, prefer to be fully Indonesian rather than Hadhramian. This is particularly true of Abdurrahman Baswedan, who in the late 1930s established the Arab-Indonesian Party (PAI).[28]

It is likely that Rizieq's journey to Saudi Arabia was directed not only towards study but also towards finding his cultural roots. He was deeply concerned about the condition of the Muslim community and the Hadhrami in particular. Soon after his return, he started wearing the *gamis* (Arab-style clothing) and turban. Like most Saudi graduates, he spoke Arabic as well Indonesian. However, Saudi Wahhabism seems to have had little influence on him for he usually identified himself as a follower of the educational tradition of Ahl al-Sunnah wal Jama'ah.[29]

As a promising young leader, Rizieq was offered a teaching post at the *madrasah aliyah* (senior Islamic high school) of Jami'at al-Khair in Tanah Abang, an area populated predominantly by Hadhrami. After some years, he was promoted to headmaster, but in 1996, he resigned from this position and remained at the Jami'at al-Khair as a teacher. In the meantime he produced a book on *tajwid* (rules of the Qur'anic recitation), *Al-Jadwal al-Mufid fi al-Ilm al-Tajwid* (The Useful List of *Tajwid*). It is said that the book was widely distributed within the *madrasah* in Indonesia, Malaysia, and Brunei.

Rizieq is an eyewitness to the changing face of Jakarta. Tanah Abang, where he grew up and became an adult, is now a slum area.[30] It is a place where prostitution and banditry are as common as the mosque and *madrasah*. Gambling and drugs have become part of the daily life of the community, together with injustice, poverty, and corruption. These realities have led to Rizieq's adoption of a no-compromise stance against illegal activities. He maintains that the flourishing of illegal activities is a sign of the state's failure to maintain law and order.

In most of his speeches, Rizieq criticizes the government for its failure to stop corruption (*kemungkaran*)[31] in the country. The Qur'anic injunction of *amr bil ma'ruf wal nahi al-munkar*—"commanding the good and forbidding the evil" (sometimes translated as "commanding righteousness and preventing corruption")—has been his main discourse theme for many years. In effect, this theme has led him to discuss such subjects as moral crisis, decadency of faith, upholding righteousness, and condemning corruption. The term *jihad* appears in most of his speeches. Before the economic crisis hit Indonesia in 1998, he had already warned the country about the dangers of the moral crisis.

The government, he argued, instead of anticipating crisis, wasted its energy on controlling public preachers.[32] A number were even jailed without clear evidence or due process because of their criticism of the government. The government censored all Muslim preachers, barring them from speaking in public unless they had previously obtained a license from the police. So it is hardly surprising that Rizieq compared Suharto to the Pharaoh, the symbol of infidelity in the Qur'an. However, he was reportedly very cautious with government officials, playing a game of cat and mouse with them.

During the 1980s and 1990s a great number of preachers took a stand against the government because of growing dissatisfaction among the *ummah*. Rizieq argued that it was time to wake up and stop making compromises. Muslim people had long been patient and tolerant, and for that they got nothing but suffering. In some instances, Muslims had been killed by the military, and in others, accused of seeking to establish an Islamic state. He held that such charges had actually been created by the elite, some of whom are Christians who view Islam as a potential threat to their interests.

THE EMERGENCE OF FRONT PEMBELA ISLAM (FPI)

On August 17, 1998, coincident with Indonesia's fifty-third anniversary commemoration, a group of preachers, *habaib*, *ustadz*, and *ulama*,[33] mostly from Jakarta, gathered in the Pesantren al-Umm, Kampung Utan Ciputat. This meeting was held to celebrate Independence Day as well as to respond to numerous issues ranging from injustice to human rights violations, in which a large number of victims were Muslims. Among the attendants were K.H. Cecep Bustami, Habib Idrus Jamalullail, K.H. Damanhuri, Habib Muhammad Rizieq Syihab, and K.H. Misbahul Anam, who was the host. In this meeting, they agreed to create an organization in which all the problems of the *ummah*, or Muslim community, could be solved. This meeting has been marked as the point of emergence of Front Pembela Islam (FPI), or Islamic Defenders Front.

The meeting attracted great interest and hundreds of Muslims attended. Some high-ranking Indonesian military officials are said to have been involved as well. The military reportedly gave a great deal of support, such as money and military training, to the FPI paramilitary members. This training was made in anticipation of emergency situations. The closeness between the military and the FPI became obvious when, at the FPI's first anniversary celebration, a number of high-ranking military officials were seen among the attendants. No less than General Djaja Suparman, the Jakarta military commander, and General Nugroho Djayoesman, the Jakarta police commander, participated in the event.[34]

Muslim leaders reacted to this relationship in different ways. Some said that this closeness was normal since the Muslims are the majority in the country. Previously the Muslim-military relationship had been suspended because the military was too close to power, and Muslims had even been used to maintain power. During the 1980s, the relationship had been at its lowest point when the military was involved in several operations that led to the loss of Muslim civilian lives. Some leaders said that although the relationship had been besieged by problems, it could be improved. According to Adi Sasono, a respected Muslim leader, the relationship between Muslims and the military was actually a dynamic phenomenon that depended on the political situation. Since the Reformasi, he claims, Muslims and the military had entered a new era, where both have opportunities to improve their relationship.[35]

Since General Faisal Tanjung's appointment as chief commander of the Indonesian military forces, important positions in the military have been controlled by Muslim generals, who, according to Olivier Roy, supported the so-called "conservative Islamism" applied by Suharto from the beginning of 1990 until his resignation in 1998.[36] Meanwhile memories of Murdani's men, a Christian and a former military commander, have gradually been erased. There emerged the so-called "green military" (Muslim generals) and "red-white military" (nationalist generals) indicating friction within the military. When the reformation took place, the military was actually handed over to the generation of General Wiranto.[37] However, it should be noted that Wiranto was appointed chief commander at a time when the military was facing many problems. Some argued that while Wiranto is actually a reformist general who was trying to restructure and reform the military, he could not single-handedly overcome all the problems facing the military, including charges of human rights violations against several generals.[38]

Another theory asserts that the military approached a number of Muslim groups to counter criticism by left-wing groups consisting of certain NGOs, intellectuals, and student associations.[39] By manipulating certain religious issues, such as the fact that the generals were Muslims, the FPI tried to shift the problem from a political one to a religious one. On many occasions, the FPI leaders have convinced the public that this was the best time to develop a mutually beneficial relationship with the military and condemned those people who criticized the military. They argued that Muslims should support the military since it was at that time controlled by Muslim generals. However, this argument did not erase the stigma of the many violations it had made in the past. People still remembered how badly the military had behaved during the 1980s, when hundreds of Muslims were killed in numerous incidents. The military's dual function had made them powerful, allowing them to control the country. In several cases, the military was accused of human rights violations. Students, NGOs, intellectuals, and human rights activists asked the government to take legal action against the generals who were behind those incidents.

It is important to note that the emergence of Muslim paramilitary groups, including the FPI, took place during the interval between Suharto's stepping down in May 1998 and the general election in 1999. Certain Muslim groups proposed that Habibie, the incumbent vice president, be given a chance at the presidency. They regarded him as a good Muslim who was genuinely concerned with Islam, as was evident in his record and his Muslim political affiliations since the beginning of the 1990s. Muslim paramilitary groups were created to mobilize and maximize the people's support. Habibie reportedly gave a huge amount of money to several Muslim groups, including the FPI, to pave the way for his presidency. His address before the members of the People's Consultative Assembly, however, was rejected; consequently, he could not stand for another presidency.[40]

K.H. Misbahul Anam, the FPI secretary-general, has doubts regarding this issue. The FPI, he said, rejected the idea of the paramilitary groups' participation as a security force during the 1999 Special Session of the People's Consultative Assembly (MPR-RI).[41] Anam believes that such participation would only have led people into conflict. While Anam cannot deny the closeness between the FPI and the military, he argues that both institutions have the task of protecting all members of the community. According to the FPI, this task does not belong exclusively to the military forces; rather all Muslims have the obligation to protect members of the community.

There are three factors underlying the emergence of the FPI. The first is the increase of *maksiat* [sinful deeds] in this country which has reached an intolerable level. It is something that we cannot [allow to] continue. We think it is necessary to make social movements that are expected to stop that *maksiat*. We can no longer rely on the government, the police officials, to do it. Otherwise we will see more and more people become victims. So we have to wake up to fight against all these things. The second factor is the growing number of human rights violations against Muslims and the impotence of the government and social and political organizations to handle all the problems. We are the majority here, but alas, from time to time we are victimized. Look at what happened in Tanjung Priok, Aceh, Haur Koneng, and Majalengka. All these incidents victimized Muslims. The third factor is that it is our obligation to perform *amr ma'ruf* and *nahi al-munkar* [command righteousness and prevent corruption] through constitutional ways existing in this country, as a step to realize the struggles of our predecessors both from NU and Muhammadiyah.[42]

Even though the FPI leaders argued that their support for the military and Habibie were based on religious grounds, no one can deny that their relationship was actually tinged with political opportunity. After the 1999 Special Session in which Habibie's address was rejected by the members of Parliament, his attempts to build relations with radical Islamic groups seem to have come to an end. Meanwhile a number of high-ranking military officials still maintained their relationship over the following years. The military needed an organization like the FPI as they continued to face several problems. Waves of demonstrations and protests against the military had become a routine part of life for the Indonesian community. The relationship between the FPI and the military, however, was really dependent upon the top military leadership and the replacement of top military leaders affected, leading some people to argue that the presence of radical Islamic groups was actually the experiment of some military officials. But this argument is too simplistic.

Since the beginning, the FPI had flourished as an independent paramilitary group aimed at protecting all the members of the Muslim community. However, it did not refuse to cooperate with any parties or groups as long as the cooperation was mutually beneficial. In this context, it is easy to understand the reason it developed a relationship with the military. If we look back to the 1980s, we can see that it was not unusual for military figures and Muslim leaders to be close. Muslim leaders, having access to the grassroots levels of the community, are always in a good bargaining position to attract certain figures, including the military.

When the FPI's relationship with the military had come to an end, Hamzah Haz, the top leader of the largest Islamic political party, the United Development Party (PPP), came into the spotlight. This relationship was partly related to the fact that the FPI is dominated by the *habaib*, who also became his party's main supporters. Hamzah needed to maintain contact with them in order to gain political access to certain Islamic groups in a broader context. He appeared to rely upon his traditional supporters for the next general election.[43] It should be pointed out that the *habaib* have important roles among the Betawinese Muslim community, the natives of the Jakarta neighborhood where the FPI is socially based. When Hamzah was elected vice president in 2001, he frequently attended meetings of both FPI and other radical Islamic groups. According to one source, Hamzah gave a great deal of support to Syihab when the FPI was facing problems.

During General Sofyan Yacob's term, the FPI experienced the worst treatment from the police. Unlike his predecessors, Yacob was not willing to tolerate any destructive acts by the FPI. From the very beginning he showed his hostility toward the group, which, he contended, has never respected the supremacy of the law. Not surprisingly, the police and the FPI paramilitary troops have been involved in a number of conflicts, the most important of which was when the FPI denied charges that Syihab had committed destructive acts. Another involved a police raid on its headquarters in Petamburan Tanah Abang following its attack on several billiard centers in West Jakarta. This raid has become a high-profile event since its occurrence. At the same time, it indicates that the support of certain high-ranking police officers has come to an end.

While most Indonesian radical Muslim groups have connections with Middle Eastern figures, the degree of their attachment depends very much on the ideological and political backgrounds underlying their foundations. The FPI's creation, however, seems to have no connection with Middle Eastern hard-line figures, even though its top leaders are graduates of the Middle Eastern institutions. The FPI was created, as was demonstrated above, to respond to the social and political situation in Indonesia; consequently, it is not surprising that it has no connection with radical Islamic groups in the Middle East. However, its very presence reportedly has attracted a number of Middle Eastern hard-line figures. No less than Osama bin Laden, the number one US enemy and the most important suspect of the September 11 terrorist attacks, is said to have offered support in the form of weapons finance. But so far, according to Misbahul Anam, the FPI does not need such support.

Circumstances are different for Laskar *Jihad* (LJ), which was founded after the issuance of a legal opinion (*fatawa*) by Middle Eastern *ulama*. Certain individuals who later became the top LJ leaders reportedly asked the opinion of some *ulama* of Yemen and Saudi Arabia concerning the Muslim-Christian conflict in Ambon.[44] The *ulama* are said to have replied that it is incumbent upon Muslims to help and protect Ambonese Muslims because of the persecution by radical Christians. The LJ was established based on this opinion, and consequently, has strong connections with its allies in the Middle East. This connection, it goes without saying, has become the *raison d'etre* for the LJ. Following the Bali bombing in October 2002 that killed hundreds of civilians, LJ leader Ja'far Umar Thalib suddenly decided to halt the LJ's activities. This decision was made after some consideration by the Middle Eastern *ulama* who said that the situation in Ambon had improved significantly so that the presence of the LJ was no longer necessary.

At the end of the 2002, there were some changes in Indonesian government policies in response to the phenomenon of radical Islamic groups. Following the October Bali bombing, the government appeared to be getting tough. One by one the leaders of radical Muslim groups were arrested by the police and charged with crimes ranging from planning to assassinate President Megawati Sukarnoputri as in the case of Abu Bakar Ba'asyir,[45] the cleric and the top leader of Majelis Mujahidin Indonesia, to contemptuous speech, as in the case of LJ leader Ja'far Umar Thalib. Syihab himself was arrested by the police and charged with the destruction of several amusement centers. Soon after this arrest, Syihab announced the dissolution of the FPI paramilitary troops because there were so many people who used them for their own political intrigues.

FPI AS A MUSLIM PARAMILITARY GROUP

From 1998 to 2000 numerous incidents occurred involving the slaughter of hundreds of so-called black magic practitioners in Java. These cases—as far as the FPI was concerned—have never been solved by the police. In response, the FPI created an independent fact-finding team (Badan Pencari Fakta), whose task was to investigate these civilian killings in several places in Java. The team went to Demak, Pasuruan, Jember, Probolinggo, and Banyuwangi. They found that the term black magic practitioner was misleading; the victims were actually members of different levels of the Muslim community and had nothing to do with black magic. The fact-finding team also learned that the motives behind all these tragedies were political and ideological.[46] The killers reportedly disguised their faces and their bodies with ninja uniforms and seemed to be well trained in doing their tasks. Some people said that such activities were aimed at creating divisions within the Muslim community. Others remarked that these were retaliatory actions by the enemies of the Muslims.

Speculation emerged among Muslim people over whether certain groups previously attacked by Muslims planned to take vengeance against them. This speculation obviously referred to communists, who were killed by Muslims following the failure of the 1965 coup d'état. Historical records indicate that thousands of members and supporters of the Indonesia Communist Party (PKI) had been killed extra-judicially by Muslims.[47] For some people like Abdurrahman Wahid, former president and the leader of the Nahdatul Ulama, whose members may have been involved in the tragedy, the 1965–1966 massacres required some kind of resolution. On many occasions he proposed the need for reconciliation between the Muslim community and PKI members and supporters. Even when he became president, the first issue he raised was Article No. 25, 1965, on communism.[48] However, this proposal only attracted public criticism and seemed to be too sophisticated for most people to comprehend. In reality, hatred of communists is still widespread.[49]

The FPI did not accuse the remnant communists of being behind the tragic killings in Java but demanded that the government capture those groups responsible for the murders. Once again, the FPI asked for the government's commitment to solving these problems. They called on the Muslim community to trust the police to take all necessary actions and to refrain from breaking the law. However, people did not seem to believe the stated intentions of the police about solving the problem, and distrust appeared to be growing. In certain places, especially in small cities and remote areas, people created paramilitary groups or voluntary security groups to protect themselves. It is not an exaggeration to say that the FPI actually pioneered the emergence of Muslim paramilitary groups. They did so because the government did not demonstrate a strong commitment to solving community problems. During the period 1998–2000, social and religious conflicts escalated and the government was very weak. Consequently, in this context, the FPI has actually become the most important movement challenging the government.

One of the most significant FPI acts was its attack on the National Commission on Human Rights (KOMNASHAM) office in Menteng Jakarta. This attack occurred following the commission's investigative report concerning the Tanjung Priok massacre in 1983,[50] in which hundreds of Muslims, as many believe, were killed. The notorious L. B. Murdani, a Christian and the chief general of the armed forces at that time, was allegedly involved. The FPI accused the commission of being unfair in conducting the investigation, which concluded that the massacre was due to *force majeur* and only a few people were killed. The FPI demanded that the government abolish the KOMNASHAM office, claiming that it was not independent in conducting its activities. From the beginning the FPI did not expect very much from it, since this commission was dominated by lawyers and human rights activists, many of whom were Christians who did not support Muslim interests.

There were also numerous attacks by the FPI on amusement centers, the most important of which was the Kemang Café in South Jakarta. Even President Abdurrahman Wahid commented on the situation, accusing the FPI of being unfair in its actions: the amusement centers that did not pay them were attacked, while others that gave them money were not. He further accused its members of having stolen expensive liquor, while cheap brands were left behind. In response, Rizieq retorted, "How did he know? He is blind, isn't he? He became aware of these accusations from his whisperers, who sometimes simply supply him with incorrect information."[51] After this event, the FPI became even more critical of Wahid and accused him of being unable to solve the country's problems.[52]

As a result of the Ketapang incident of November 1998, the FPI emerged into public awareness for the first time. According to an FPI investigation, the incident began when a group of young Ambonese tortured a young Muslim boy named Irfan. His father, Udin, came to the site of the incident and asked his son what had happened. Instead of receiving an explanation, Udin was tortured and sent to the hospital. The situation spun out of control. A group of about a hundred Christians flocked to the location and burned down a mosque. The Ketapang community, mostly Batavian Muslims, called the FPI headquarters in Petamburan, and by the time the FPI paramilitary troops arrived, the two opposing groups were ready for a war. The FPI controlled the situation and prevented further trouble.

The following week violence took place in Kupang, the capital of the predominantly Christian province of East Nusa Tenggara. It was obvious that the violence was prompted by the Ketapang incident. A large number of Christian groups began the day by thronging in the streets and burning down every mosque they could find. A dozen Muslims were reportedly killed. One source said that the incident was provoked by General Theo Syafei, the Balinese military commander, and his voice was recorded as evidence of his involvement in the incident. A number of Muslim groups demanded that the government charge Syafei and arrest him.[53]

On December 1, the FPI released a strong statement on the Kupang incident. First, it condemned the actions of the Christian groups for killing and torturing Muslims and for demolishing and burning the mosques. Second, the FPI called on all Christians in the country to refrain from any violent acts that might anger Muslims. Third, the FPI demanded that the government investigate the Kupang incident and punish those responsible for it. Fourth, it called on all Muslims to engage in *jihad* to defend the majesty of Islam.[54]

Like many other Islamic fundamentalist groups, the FPI also sent their soldiers to Ambon to help the Moluccan Muslims to fight against the Christians. The Moluccan battlefield, as an eyewitness soldier called it, was a *jihad* where the soldiers longed for martyrdom (*shahid*). They believed that the Ambon tragedy was, in fact, an international conspiracy to divide Indonesia into separate countries, some of which would be controlled by the Western-affiliated Christians. Therefore, they felt it was incumbent upon all Muslims to defend their country. Some sources claimed that the Forum for Moluccan Sovereignty (FKM) was controlled by radical Christians, whose plan was to build an independent state for Ambonese Christians. The forum is actually the remnant of the previously known separatist movement, the South Moluccan Republic (RMS), led by Dr. Soumokil at the beginning of Indonesian independence, which aimed to separate the South Moluccas from Indonesia. While this movement has since dispersed, remnants of it can still be found there. Ambon is one of the most critical regions in Indonesia where Muslims and Christian have frequently been involved in conflicts.

According to available information, the FPI sent only a small number of troops. It is reported that the group's flag was hoisted along with that of the LJ,[55] which sent a large number of military personnel. LJ has not only been involved in military actions, it has also engaged in humanitarian and community development activities.[56] It brought in doctors, paramedics, teachers, and social workers working side by side with members of the community. The Ambon conflict never became a major concern for the FPI. As we shall see in the following section, the FPI has focused its activities on social issues particularly related to *amr bil ma'ruf wal nahi al-munkar* (commanding righteousness and preventing corruption).

However, the FPI has also taken an interest in global political issues, particularly the Israeli-Palestinian conflict and US foreign policies towards Muslim countries. This concern was manifested in its rejection of the presence of the Israeli delegation during the International Parliamentary Union conference held in Jakarta in 2000. The FPI threatened to deploy itself in Jakarta and siege Sukarno-Hatta Airport if the organizing committee of the conference insisted on inviting the Israeli delegation.

The FPI has also been involved in anti-American activities following the US attacks on Afghanistan and Iraq. Most Muslims believe that these attacks are not justifiable since the two countries under siege are independent, sovereign nations. These attacks, they say, have also proven that the United States is actually a terrorist country that does not respect human rights and democracy. Together with students, intellectuals, NGOS, women activists, and human rights activists, the FPI demonstrated at the US embassy in Jakarta, shouting anti-American slogans. Its leaders also vowed to sweep Jakarta and expel all the Americans from the city.[57] Concern over Afghanistan and Iraq has made a number of Islamic organizations, including the FPI, organize a commission that helps send volunteers to these two countries. Rizieq planned to fly to Amman, the capital of Jordan, for humanitarian aid programs in the last minutes before the first US bomb was dropped in Baghdad even though he was under house arrest.

The fact that the FPI promotes anti-American sentiment in the country does not mean that it is anti-West.[58] The group simply refuses to accept secular ideas and Western domination. As long as the world remains in an unbalanced state, and as long as other powers remain dominant in the

Muslim world, Muslims will wage *jihad*, the so-called martyrdom or *shahid* that every Muslim longs for. According to the FPI, Western domination is only possible because the West, especially the United States, controls the global political situation through several international bodies, including the United Nations and the IMF. These bodies, the FPI believes, are the subordinates of US foreign policy.

AMR BIL MA'RUF WAL NAHI AL-MUNKAR—
THE MOVEMENT TO COMMAND RIGHTEOUSNESS
AND PREVENT CORRUPTION

The FPI's emergence has created the image of radical Islam in Indonesia. This image is acknowledged by its leaders who, according to Ahmad Shabri Lubis, share the tasks and responsibilities with other Muslim groups, most of which focus on education, *dakwah* (religious propagation and enlightenment), and social activism. Since none of these other groups focus on *amr bil ma'ruf* (commanding righteousness) and *nahi al-munkar* (preventing corruption) issues, FPI members take on these activities, even though they might risk their lives in doing so.

Commanding righteousness and preventing corruption are actually the responsibility of every Muslim. If Muhammadiyah or Nahdatul Ulama carried out these activities, the FPI would be unnecessary. The FPI was created because no one else was assuming these responsibilities. There is an apparent division of labor among Indonesian Muslim groups. The Muhammadiyah is active in education and social activities, while the NU works in traditional Islamic education, supporting thousands of Islamic boarding schools throughout the country. The same also holds true for the Indonesian Commission for Islamic Mission (DDII), whose concerns revolve around *dakwah*. Their *dakwah* are not only in the cities or in the villages, but also in very remote areas, in the mountains and jungles. They anticipate and intercept Christian missionaries and are the only group that can do this. The FPI sees in this division of labor a remaining gap regarding *amr bil ma'ruf wal nahi al-munkar*. Apart from the FPI, no other group is taking on the responsibility of destroying *kemaksiatan* (corruption), because it is very difficult. Ahmad Shabri Lubis explained, "We fight against criminals and gangsters. Sometimes we confront the officials. We don't care what people say about us. The terms *radical* or *militant* do not really matter."[59]

31

The model of Islam as exemplified by the FPI has intensified radical Islamic movements in Indonesia. This phenomenon can be seen in Jakarta and the surrounding areas. Several Muslim groups in Tangerang, Depok, Bogor, and Bekasi have been influenced by the FPI to varying degrees and many have even joined the organization and established new branches in their locations, causing a snowball effect in the growing number of members and supporters. Misbahul Anam claims that FPI members and supporters during the group's first years totaled around 15 million people, with branches in seventeen provinces throughout the country.[60]

While Anam may have exaggerated in his estimate, it is obvious that the FPI has its own way of getting the support of Muslim groups. It introduces the simple idea that every Muslim has the obligation "to command righteousness and prevent corruption." This doctrine has actually been applied by several Muslim groups but none has ever used it as the FPI has, to attract lower-class urban Muslims who have been socially and religiously deprived.[61] Its ability to develop solidarity among them is what has made the movement massive and popular. The sense of obligation is turned into the spirit of resistance. Like a doubled-edge sword, it is used to fight both the enemies of God and the wealthy, who, the FPI contends, waste their money on evil practices.

It is common knowledge that there are many places in Jakarta, Tangerang, Bogor, and Bekasi where prostitution, drugs, and gambling exist under the guise of legal businesses. The FPI argues that the businesses, besides being illegal, have created numerous problems. According to the Perda (regional rules) of Jakarta No. 19, 1985, public entertainment places are allowed to remain open only until 2:00 a.m. However, the rule has never been enforced and these places remain open until 5:00 a.m. To solve this problem, the FPI has suggested that the government create an anti-*kemaksiatan* act to regulate the pubs, discotheques, bars, and casinos that are mushrooming in virtually every corner of the city. Given the fact that the government is not serious in enforcing the law, the FPI takes on this responsibility as a form of dark justice. However, it is fully aware that destructive actions are against the law, so it usually sends notices to the entertainment center owners warning them to obey the rules. If the owners refuse to comply, it attacks the establishments.[62]

This kind of *dakwah* is justified by Islam,[63] according to the FPI, which maintains that it practices it to enforce the law. Actually the FPI prefers dialogue rather than destructive acts and believes that corrupt officials represent Indonesia's greatest law enforcement problem. It is generally known that they accept bribes from businessmen whom they allow to break the law.[64] For this reason, the FPI views Indonesia as a mafia republic actually controlled by gangsters, criminals, and corrupt officials.[65] Law enforcement, it maintains, is merely an illusion.

Although other Muslim organizations as well as the general public have criticized this kind of *dakwah*, the FPI does not seem concerned. It argues that many other Muslim organizations have become impotent after receiving donations from foreign funding agencies that carry political strings. As a result, these organizations do not appear to care about social issues. Meanwhile, there have been some claims that the FPI has actually been involved in blackmail activities against the owners of entertainment businesses.[66]

The FPI has established standard procedures in taking action, adhering to the Qur'anic injunction to carry out the *dakwah* "with wisdom, good preaching, and polite discussions."[67] On many occasions the FPI gives input to the local authorities concerning the growing *kemaksiatan* and drug abuse. It is frequently invited by local authorities to discuss certain social and religious issues as well as those concerning the fasting month of Ramadan. In certain regions, local authorities even invite the FPI to discuss the formation of local laws. Working together with other Islamic organizations, it proposes drafts of these laws. However, these activities have never been covered by the media, which are more tempted to write about sensational issues. So people are simply ignorant about the FPI's activities because they are not informed.

The FPI divides the offending entertainment places into two categories: *nahi al-munkar and amr bil m'aruf*. The category of *nahi al-munkar* ("preventing corruption") refers to places where the FPI believes *kemungkaran* activities could be eradicated without leading to horizontal conflicts. The category of *amr bil ma'ruf* ("commanding righteousness") on the other hand, refers to places that cannot be targeted for the corruption prevention program as this would only lead to horizontal conflicts. Instead, the FPI will encourage its people to hold programs focusing on community development and Islamic teachings. If the people in such places are not supportive or if they deny the existence of such *kemungkaran*, the FPI will target such places as *nahi al-munkar* and take action against them.

Moreover, it should be noted that the FPI follows a specific list of procedures before taking action. First, together with the local people, it drafts a resolution that the people sign, stating that they refuse all *kemungkaran* in their neighborhood. The FPI presents this resolution to the local authorities and the businessmen who run such places. If within two weeks there is no response either from the local authorities or the businessmen, it takes action.

> Illegal practices are intolerable. When the authorities respond to our notices and warnings, the problem is over. Why should we waste time and energy chartering buses and mobilizing people? We are not paid anyway. We pay them. That's their job. We support them to be more active. We want them do their jobs. That's all. When they do their job, the problem is solved. But when our warnings are not heeded, we report to the higher authorities. We ask them to handle these problems. Everything is procedural. We are good citizens. We have to stress that. If the higher authorities respond to our report and handle the problems, then the problem is over. You can see our procedures—how patient we are. We do not destroy the places suddenly. We obey the law. But if the law doesn't work, what happens then?

When water is unchanneled, what happens? It floods everywhere. We can flood the city.[68]

It is interesting that the FPI does not use the term "law enforcement," but rather *gusur kemaksiatan* (destroy the corruption). For most Muslims, "law enforcement" is too difficult to understand; "destroy the corruption" is easier, even though it implies the dark style of justice. Moreover, it has specific connotations that can arouse religious sentiments. *Maksiat* has been a sensitive issue among Muslims as it refers to immoral activities that violate religious teachings. By using such jargon as *gusur maksiat* and *ganyang munkarat*[69] (destroy the corruption), the FPI mobilizes the masses and summons them for *jihad*. Most of its members understand *jihad* as the attempt to perform all religious duties and defend the dignity of Islam, even with destructive acts. Those Muslims who perform these duties will be forgiven by God as they are true believers.

Kemaksiatan is an extremely important issue during Ramadan, when the FPI intensifies its activity. Some radical Muslim groups have manipulated the issue to achieve their political gains. The FPI, together with other Muslim groups, mobilize in Jakarta and gather at Monas Square to encourage the public to fight against *kemaksiatan* and ask the government and non-Muslims to respect Muslims.[70] Working with its branches and allies, it makes the entire month a field of *jihad*. After performing *shalat tarawih* (supplementary prayer during the nights of Ramadan), its members begin their activities, targeting pubs, casinos, bars, and discotheques. They stop at the time of *sahur*, the predawn meal, around three to four in the morning.

Movements against *maksiat* are not limited to Jakarta, but also take place in Bogor, about fifty miles away, where Muslim leaders have expressed their concerns and suggested that local authorities limit public entertainment activities during Ramadan. In Puncak, a large, mountainous tourist resort, there are about a hundred public entertainment places that are allegedly used for prostitution. Although several Muslim communities in this area have voiced their distress and concern, the local authorities cannot do anything since Puncak brings a great deal of money to the region through tourism.

Still another, similar, entertainment center is located at Parung, about fifteen miles from Jakarta, where the FPI once attacked a number of bars, karaokes, and pubs. Many believe that there are also places that offer prostitution. At the same time, parts of this area, particularly Sawangan and Depok, are home to several Islamic boarding schools and mosques as part of the Islamization movements that have emerged since the 1980s.[71] When the FPI was established in 1998, a number of Muslim leaders from this area stated their allegiance as they found that it was what they had been waiting for. Depok and Sawangan have been known as FPI's strongest branches and several times have actually warned bars, karaokes, and pubs to close during Ramadan. When this warning went unheeded, they attacked the businesses.

During the period 1998–2000, while people were caught up in the euphoria of democracy, a number of events took place that had never before been imagined. People were exposed to pornography on such a large scale that it raised protest and concern in communities. The FPI was involved in activities to fight *kemaksiatan* and support the participation of communities in this fight. The FPI reportedly encouraged the Kebon Melati community to close several places that were allegedly used for prostitution and gambling and supported the Rawa Buaya community in East Jakarta in its effort to close similar places.

IDEOLOGY OF FPI

The FPI's goal is to guarantee Islamic law for Muslims in Indonesia. It holds that Islam and the state cannot be separated from each other. The state was created to protect all the people and grant them rights. According to the FPI, the implementation of Islamic teachings is one of the civil rights that should be granted by the state.[72] If Islamic teachings were implemented, the Indonesian people would live in peace and prosperity. Islamic fundamentalist movements always view adversity and crisis as God's punishment for the absence of Islamic law in the Muslim people's daily lives. Thus, the multi-dimensional crisis facing Indonesia is believed to be a consequence of Indonesia's Western-affiliated politics and economics along with the adoption of secular laws, which are in fact inappropriate for Indonesians.

To attain the goal of implementing *shariah*, the FPI created the National Commission for the Application of Islamic Law. The commission's task is to advocate the use of Islamic law to its members as well as to other Muslim people. Local commissions were created in several provinces in the country, where the concept of Islamic law is further introduced at the grassroots levels. According to the FPI, Muslims have responded to these programs positively.[73] At the grassroots level, appreciation of Islamic law or *shariah* remains alive in the people's consciousness. The FPI believes that the reason for the positive response is that secular law does not fit the people's aspirations.

The fact that Muslims remain supportive of Islamic law is verified by a national survey conducted by the Center for the Study of Islam and Society (PPIM) in 2001 and 2000, indicating that Muslims' support for Islamic law is relatively high.[74] But these statistics do not necessarily satisfy Islamic law opponents. When people are asked specific questions concerning the application of Islamic law (for example, punishments like cutting off the hands of thieves and stoning adulterers to death, as found in classical Islamic legal texts), the percentage of supporters drops significantly, indicating that people have different understandings of what *shariah* really is. Historically, *shariah* has never been clearly understood. Muslims basically do not question *shariah* when it is concerned with general Islamic principles. However, when it is understood as *fiqh* or jurisprudence involving specific details of crimes and punishments, then there is disagreement.

Even though it is difficult to implement *shariah*, the FPI claims to have succeeded in promoting this idea. In some regions in Java as well as in Sumatra, Sulawesi, and Kalimantan, Islamic law has actually been applied. In Cianjur, West Java, for instance, the so-called Gerbang Marhamah (the Gate of Blessing) movement has been campaigning for Islamic law.[75] Movements like this are said to have the support of both the public and local authorities. Muslim leaders in Cianjur reportedly have prepared a draft of Islamic law on a national scale. *Shariah* movements are also found in Makassar, Padang, and Serang Banten, communities known to have the most strongly committed Muslims in Indonesia. So far, however, these movements have been elitist, appealing only to particular segments of the community.

Moreover, in many cases, the application of *shariah* appears to be more symbolic than substantial, which sometimes causes skepticism among its opponents. What is meant by *shariah* is sometimes equated with veiling for women, having women escorted by their *muhrim* while traveling, etc.—issues that gender activists have criticized. In some cases, *shariah* is even understood as having a long beard and wearing the *koko*, a Javanese traditional clothing style for men. In Aceh, however, *shariah* also has political and cultural manifestations, since the province has long been in conflict with the government over the right to have Islam as its cultural and political identity. These diverse examples indicate that among the *shariah* proponents themselves, the term is subject to different interpretations.

Unlike some other proponents of Islamic law, the FPI interprets *shariah* in a more substantive way; it proposes that certain ideas derived from Islamic teachings be integrated into national law. Thus it has prepared several drafts and proposals. For instance, it has suggested that an anti-*maksiat* act be instituted and implemented since *maksiat* has become a social disease not only within the Muslim community but also among non-Muslims. It has already drafted the act, as well as others regarding drugs, *zakat* (almsgiving), the *hajj* (pilgrimage), and Islamic criminal law.[76] The FPI has never been involved in *jilbab* or *koko* movements despite the fact that its members' uniform resembles traditional Arab clothing.

In spite of its destructive acts and expressions of frustration and anger towards law enforcement, the FPI has actually become a viable challenge to national law enforcement. Since the beginning of the Reformasi, law enforcement and the national legal system have become crucial issues of debate. On the one hand, there appears to be some agreement that there are many weaknesses in the national legal system directly related to the low quality of law enforcement. On the other hand, the government's political will and the concrete steps it has taken to reform this system remain far from adequate, leading to public skepticism over its ability and willingness to achieve reform.

Some argue that the national legal system can be reformed by improving the existing structure and apparatus. It is important to note that the present system has been adopted from the colonial legal system established by the Netherlands, which is regarded as no longer appropriate for modern Indonesia. Many Muslim leaders argue that Islamic law can make a significant contribution to the national legal system. They feel that because of the openness afforded by the 1998 reformation, the time is ripe to make such changes. The FPI is willing to participate in this process by campaigning for the application of Islamic law, which it argues, should be integrated into national law and be enforceable only for Muslims.

The FPI leaders realize that legal reform would take a great deal of time and energy. They believe in the gradual principle (*tadarruj*) in the process of *jihad*. As they say, it is not like eating chili pepper and then feeling hot. The goal at the moment is to provide a national legal framework within which Islamic law could be integrated. Whether Islamic law is applied in the coming "five years, ten years, fifty years, one hundred years, or even five thousand years, does not really matter. The important thing is that we go through all the processes, and provide all the supporting factors for the application of Islamic law."[77]

Muslims' expectations regarding Islamic law appear to support universal human rights and should not be interpreted as threatening to non-Muslims. If non-Muslims need a legal system derived from their own tradition or religion, the government should give them the same treatment as it does Muslims. However, some secular Muslim intellectuals—usually graduates of Western universities—and Islamophobic non-Muslims have created anxieties among Muslims and non-Muslims about the application of Islamic law. Consequently, the movement has lost some momentum.

The FPI nonetheless predicts that through the government's autonomy program, one by one the provinces in which Muslims are the majority will choose Islamic law instead of secular law. For the final phase, the FPI proposes that a national referendum be held to decide whether Islamic law should be applied on a national scale. If the majority of Indonesian people vote for Islamic law, it should be applied nationally, and if they vote for secular law, Islamic law could only be applied in those provinces in which the majority vote for it. Habib Muhammad Rizieq Syihab, FPI's chief leader, believes that the majority would vote for Islamic law.[78]

According to the FPI, the application of Islamic law does not necessarily mean the establishment of an Islamic state. There is no verse in the Qur'an requiring Muslims to establish an Islamic state, while one can easily find verses stating that Muslims should follow the law of God. The FPI's proposal for the application of Islamic law thus does not oppose the Republic of Indonesia (RI). Its allegiance to the RI appears to be beyond question. At its founding on August 17, 1998, the FPI insisted that its members were "true believers" in the RI. In its early years, its website had a statement (no longer available) that, the FPI believes, is derived from the Prophet's sayings: "The Prophet has foretold that at the end of the era, his country would emerge in this world with a red and white flag." Allegiance to the Republic of Indonesia (whose flag is red and white) is integrated into FPI teachings and is recorded in many of its documents, including the so-called Decree on Women's Appointment as President.[79] This decree contains an oath to guard the unity of the Republic of Indonesia and its security, order, and safety. On many occasions this oath of allegiance has been a ritual part of FPI activities.

Consequently, it is hard to imagine that the FPI would oppose the RI, which is, in fact, the *raison d'etre* for the FPI's establishment. Every year on Independence Day, thousands of FPI members flock to the city bringing red and white flags, as do other Indonesians. Other radical Islamic groups like Laskar *Jihad* (the Soldiers of *Jihad*) and the United Actions of the Indonesian Muslim Students (KAMMI) have never been involved in this patriotic celebration. The FPI has never questioned the presence of the RI. This is one of its main characteristics, which differentiates it from other groups, such as the Hizbut Tahrir (the Party of Liberty), whose ultimate goal is to create an Islamic caliphate.

To the FPI it does not really matter whether the RI is an Islamic state or a Pancasila state as long as it gives Muslims the opportunity to live in accordance with Islamic teachings. The FPI argues that to live with and practice Islamic teachings is the right of every Muslim; the state should guarantee this right since it was founded to guarantee the rights of its citizens. If the state does not guarantee these rights, or if it limits or constrains them, it is not living up to its ultimate goals. According to the FPI, this is what happened in the past when the state did not guarantee Muslims the right to live with Islamic teachings. As a result, Muslims at various times have demanded that the government give them the opportunity to implement Islamic teachings. It is hardly surprising that the relationship between Muslims and the state has been filled with tension and conflict, particularly in the early years of Indonesian history. A notable example is Darul Islam (the Abode of Islam), an archetypal Islamic movement that opposed Jakarta because of dissatisfaction over various issues, including the absence of the state's guarantee to apply Islamic law. The FPI argues:

We don't really care about the form of the state. Whether it is an Islamic state or a Pancasila state, we don't care. The important thing is that Muslims live in peace. Muslims should be respected because we deserve some respect. That's all. I want to tell you something. If we live in Singapore, we are the minority. If we live in the United States, we are the minority. Would it be possible to call for *shariah* as the state legal system there in those countries? That would be impossible because Muslims are the minority. It would be stupid to do that if you are the minority. But here, we are 90 percent of the entire population. We are asking for something that we deserve to have; we are asking for something that is possible. That's all. So don't try to make any outrageous interpretations.[80]

According to Martin van Bruinessen, Muslim dissatisfaction was also represented in the emergence of Masyumi, another archetype of radical Islam in Indonesia. Before it was banned in the late 1950s, Masyumi, the largest Islamic party of the Sukarno period, attempted to make Islam the ideology of the state. However, this effort came to an end when Sukarno issued a decree dismissing the Parliament and returning to the UUD '45, the 1945 Constitution. At that time Indonesia had a liberal political system that eventually became politically fragmented and socially regimented. In some parts of the country, separatist movements became serious threats to national integration. Masyumi was eventually banned because Sukarno believed that a number of its top leaders had been involved in the Revolutionary Government of the Republic of Indonesia movement (PRRI) in Sumatra. In the late 1950s, Sukarno banned all ideological and political movements and proposed the Guided Democracy policy, in which democracy was actually reduced to an authoritarian state. In spite of the official ban on Masyumi, memories of it remained alive and transformed it into new organizations. A number of newly born Islamic organizations during the Suharto era grew out of nostalgia for Masyumi. Among these are the Parmusi (Indonesian Muslim Party) and the Indonesian Commission for Islamic Mission (DDII). The former was a political party that, in the early 1970s, together with other Islamic parties, was fused into the United Development Party (PPP), an Islamic party that rivaled Golkar, the New Order's political machine. The DDII was an organization focused on Islamic missionary activities, including intercepting Christian missionary pursuits in remote areas.

Martin van Bruinessen's theoretical framework, however, is unable to explain the existence of the FPI, which is ideologically and politically associated with neither Darul Islam nor Masyumi.[81] It is simply the expression of Muslims' dissatisfaction with law enforcement in Indonesia. Its roots can be found in various social movements of the 1980s and 1990s, when modernization with all its ramifications began to spread throughout the country. Many people, especially in the urban areas, not necessarily Muslims, began to be concerned about their environment, which had deteriorated because of the negative impacts of modernization. Consequently, since the 1980s, a number of anti-drug and anti-alcoholism movements have emerged in many cities sometimes leading to radical activities. These movements are supported by most of the community members working side by side with the police. On many street corners one can see their banners emblazoned with statements like "Say no to drugs," "This is a drug-free area," "Watch out, you drug users!" which reflect concern and even anger regarding social problems. In several areas, they have taken action against drug dealers and users.[82]

Meanwhile, numerous other Muslim groups have also been deeply concerned about drug use, alcoholism, pornography, prostitution, and gambling, as these issues are related to their religious beliefs. I argue that movements to control these activities were primarily social movements. Only later did Muslims, especially the mosque-based youth associations, incorporate religious sentiments. Time and again they took action against places that were considered un-Islamic. Later these movements were represented by the FPI, which apparently manipulated social movements in the public life as another reason to justify its existence. Alcoholism, narcotics, pornography, and prostitution are social problems; finding solutions to them is the responsibility of all members of the community. The FPI, however, combines these social problems with religious sentiments to gain legitimacy and support.

Islamism is the central point of the FPI. Islamism is defined as a set of ideas asserting the need for Islam to be implemented in the form of political and legal principles. The FPI does not have sophisticated ideologies, unlike other radical Islamic groups like Hizbut Tahrir's idea of the caliphate or the Muslim Brotherhood's concept of the Muslim community epitomized by the *ummah*. If we look at the qualifications of the FPI members, it is obvious that their Islamism is very much like that of other Muslim people in general. According to the FPI's general rules, its members should perform *salat* (prayer) five times a day, observe fasting during the month of Ramadan, learn about Islam, and behave in accordance with Islamic teachings—a set of values practiced by other Muslims. During my visits to FPI headquarters in 1999–2000, I saw nothing special about them, which surprised me. Unlike members of the LJ, who are highly organized and disciplined, FPI members appear easy-going and most of them even smoked. These characteristics, superficial as they are, suggest that the FPI's ideological underpinnings and discipline are really quite simple.

Even though the FPI is not connected to the earlier Masyumi and Darul Islam movements, it has used some matters of historical precedence to gain legitimacy. On many occasions, its leaders claim that the application of *shariah* is actually legitimate and is historically guaranteed. Clearly, what they mean by historical precedence is that crucial segment of Indonesian history during which democracy has seemed to have been hijacked. Prior to Indonesia's official attainment of independence on August 17, 1945, the founding fathers, representing both Muslim and nationalist factions, had come to agree that Muslims must be given every opportunity to practice Islamic teachings in their life. The document stipulating this idea, the Jakarta Charter, was canceled following alleged criticism by Christian leaders who did not agree with the stipulation. This cancellation became the factor that sometimes triggered physical conflicts between Muslim people and the state. The Jakarta Charter issue remains problematic and seems to be unresolved even now.

THE JAKARTA CHARTER AND ISLAMIC LAW

In 1942, Japan occupied Indonesia, replacing the Dutch, who had ruled it as a colony for 350 years. The majority of Indonesian people welcomed their arrival as they promised to set Indonesia free from Dutch colonialism. On April 1945, the Japanese established the so-called Dokuritsu Jumbi Chosakai (Investigative Commission on Preparatory Attempts at Indonesia's Independence, BPUPKI) and Dokuritsu Jumbi Junkai (Preparatory Commission on Indonesia's Independence, PPKI), whose tasks were to make all the preparations and take all the necessary steps leading to independence. These bodies consisted of Indonesian leaders from both secular and Muslim factions.

From May 29 to June 1, 1945 the BPUPKI created the Commission of Nine: Sukarno, Mohammad Hatta, A. A. Maramis, Abikusno Tjokrosujoso, Abdul Kahar Muzakkir, Haji Agus Salim, Ahmad Subardjo, K.H. Abdul Wahid Hasyim, and Muhammad Yamin. Its tasks were to discuss state philosophy and the national constitution. In June 1945, it produced the Jakarta Charter, a gentlemen's agreement between Muslims and secular factions on these issues.[83] Pancasila (the Five Principles) is based on secular principles.[84] Considering the fact that Muslims are the majority in this country, the Jakarta Charter gave them the opportunity to carry out their religious practices.

The Jakarta Charter consists of two documents, the Preamble and the Pancasila. To the Pancasila's first principle, Belief in One God, the Jakarta Charter added *"dengan kewajiban menjalankan syari'at Islam bagi pemeluk-pemeluknya"* (with the obligation for Muslims to observe Islamic law), later called the "seven words" which clearly guarantee the application of Islamic law for Muslims. This phrase is also found in the Constitution, Article 29. This agreement could have been accepted by both factions, Muslim and secular. But these words were removed the very next day of Indonesia's independence, August 18, 1945, when Sukarno and Hatta decreed that Pancasila and the Constitution of 1945 were the state philosophy and national constitution, respectively. The phrases explaining the guarantee of the application of Islamic law were annulled. This deletion reportedly was made in response to opposition from the Christian factions who argued that if Muslims insisted on including these "seven words," they would secede from the nation and create their own country in the eastern part of Indonesia. Muhammad Hatta was the first person who reportedly supported this deletion, believing that these phrases would only lead to the country's disintegration.[85]

Obviously, the annulment raised opposition from Muslim factions. A number of Muslim leaders argue that the Jakarta Charter is an authentic document regarding the formulation of the national constitution, which had been produced in constitutional ways. Its annulment is believed to have been the first betrayal of democracy-building. During the period 1945–1955, several movements sprang up that, by and large, had been instigated by the debate on Islam's position in the national context. The Darul Islam rebellion, which broke out in the late 1950s and early 1960s, is evidence of how Islam remained a central issue in the political life of certain Muslim groups. The rebellion was an expression of their disillusionment with the national political situation, which was not supportive of their aspirations.

In 1955, the first fair general election was held and Indonesia entered the parliamentary era. During the period 1955–1959, there were many opportunities for Muslim factions to discuss Islam as a political ideology.[86] However, Muslim factions in the Parliament, represented by Masyumi and Nahdatul Ulama, did not have a majority as they were slightly outnumbered by the nationalist secular faction, represented by the PNI (Indonesian National Party) and the PKI (Indonesian Communist Party). Consequently, the parliamentary sessions always became deadlocked. In response to this situation, President Sukarno on July 5, 1959 issued a decree to return to the Constitution of 1945. This decree made it much more difficult, if not impossible, for Islam to be the state ideology.

Although the Jakarta Charter has been neglected during the last sixty years, its spirit lives on in the consciousness of some Muslim groups. During the New Order era this issue remained dormant. But since the beginning of the Reformasi period, many Muslims have raised the issue of reviving the Jakarta Charter and a new debate has begun. A number of Islamic parties, including the United Development Party (PPP), Crescent Party (PBB), and Justice Party (PK), have been its staunchest supporters. And during every annual session of the People's Consultative Assembly (MPR), the issue has been raised as an agenda item. Given that the majority in Parliament does not support it, during the 2001 process of amending the national constitution, these groups called for the amendment of Article 29 of the Constitution. This article, they argue, should include the "seven words" that stipulate the application of Islamic law.

Habib Muhammad Rizieq Syihab has written an important book on this issue, *Dialog Piagam Jakarta*,[87] reportedly in response to requests from his colleagues and friends. Because of the FPI's concern with the Jakarta Charter, his colleagues and friends suggested that he write a book explaining all the problems of this document so that they will be more easily understood by the public.

In this book, Rizieq demonstrates that the skepticism and cynicism of the opponents of Islamic law are really groundless; if applied, Islamic law will only be valid for Muslims. Since freedom of religious life is guaranteed under the Constitution, Muslims should be given the opportunity to live and practice their religious teachings. In most of his speeches, Rizieq states that the FPI supports those political parties whose platforms include the application of Islamic law at the national level. For Rizieq, the Jakarta Charter is only an entry point whereby the public can discuss and explore again the visibility of Islamic law and its integration into the national legal system. However, these attempts have been opposed, surprisingly, by some

Muslim intellectuals,[88] usually secular or Western-minded intellectuals, who see the issue of the Jakarta Charter as a Pandora's box.[89]

Rizieq argues that the document is important because it records one of the most important events in the formulation of the national constitution. It is the legal-constitutional basis for the application of Islamic law since it was produced by a commission in which both Muslim and nationalist factions were fairly represented. He points out that, according to Sukarno, the Jakarta Charter inspired the framing of the national constitution, and these two documents cannot be separated from each other. But so far this issue has not attracted the majority of Indonesians.

ORGANIZATION AND SOCIAL BASES OF FPI

To better understand how the FPI operates on a daily basis, it is important to shed some light on its organizational structure and division of responsibilities. Structurally, it consists of two parts: the consultative assembly (*majlis syuro*) and the executive board. The former consists of a number of respected people whose main tasks are to give advice to the executive board. It is the highest body in the organization. Of its five members, one is appointed as its chief leader (*ketua dewan majlis syuro*). To undertake its duties, the *majlis syuro* is supported by five commissions: the commissions of *shariah*, honor, coordination, consultancy, and supervision.

The executive board is involved in the organization's day-to-day affairs and runs the organization based on the mandate given by the *majlis syuro*. The board is headed by a chief leader, currently Muhammad Rizieq Syihab, and a secretary-general, currently Ahmad Shabri Lubis.[90] To manage its activities, the executive has twelve departments: foreign affairs; home affairs; religious affairs; *jihad* and state defense; social, political, and legal affairs; education and culture; economy and industry; research and technology; logistics; social welfare; information; and women's affairs. The secretary-general is supported by six special commissions: FPI experts, FPI recruitment, FPI investigation, FPI legal assistance, anti–*maksiat*, and anti-violence.

The FPI has branches at the national, provincial, regional, district, and semi-district levels. Because of the organization's large size, it appears to face problems of internal coordination and consolidation, which lead to fragmentation within its networks. Many of its branches seem closely coordinated with the central office; however, in central Java, the FPI Surakarta claims to be independent and has nothing to do with Jakarta.[91] This situation indicates that FPI faces many problems in its organizational network. Meanwhile, its strongest bases appear to coincide with the pattern of Hadhrami settlements, which are scattered in Java's northern cities. FPI is particularly strong in the northern cities of West Java, such as Bekasi, Karawang, and Subang, and in some cities in the western parts of Central Java, especially Brebes, Tegal, and Pemalang. It is also active in certain inland cities of West Java that have Hadhrami settlements such as Bogor, Depok, and Sukabumi, particularly during Ramadan.

The FPI is an open organization; anyone can become a member or supporter. This indicates that it is not a clandestine movement like Darul Islam, which always kept a certain distance from the people. It is this aspect that has made the FPI grow so rapidly but ineffectively. In a number of places, certain FPI members have been involved in blackmail activities that are usually carried out by the vigilantes. However, it is misleading to assume that the FPI is simply "a racket or mob for hire" by political manipulators, as some of its critics have charged.[92] This assumption is clearly groundless, for even today, when many of its political patrons have abandoned it, the FPI still remains active in numerous places.

When the FPI emerged at the grassroots level in 1998, its main supporters were the *ulama, kyai,* and *ustadz,* who give religious teachings to Muslim people with no material compensation. They have a traditional network with the *habaib.* It is not an exaggeration to say that the village religious leaders, or *kyai kampung,* as Habib Rizieq calls them, have become important elements in the FPI movement.

The *kyai kampung* (village religious scholars) are *ulama* and *kyai* (preachers) who are unknown to most people They give religious teachings, from one mosque to another, from one village to another. Their insights are as sharp as knives and swords. Watch out when they get angry. They are angry because of Allah, not because of their low desires. Their hearts are beating. The hearts of their students and followers are also beating, waiting for the command of *jihad,* which can happen at any time. If the drums of war have been beaten by those consistent *ulama,* if the commands of *jihad* have been announced by the *kyai* of the Hereafter, the Muslim people would come like a flock of birds, welcoming the *jihad* and waiting for His forgiveness. They are the soldiers of Allah, who are ready to meet death with smiles and happiness. "Live with dignity or die as a *syuhada* (martyr)."[93]

If there is anything that frightens the FPI, it is the Laskar Pembela Islam (Islamic Defenders Paramilitary or LPI), which is a part of the FPI organization attached to the departments of *jihad* and state defense. It is this group that usually organizes demonstrations and undertakes destructive acts against entertainment places. The FPI paramilitary group has an organizational structure that is very much like that of the military. It is led by the chief commander who is Rizieq himself, and has a hierarchical command structure. The members of this paramilitary group are selected through a system of recruitment that focuses on physical skills, since martial arts and mental discipline are part of their regimen. They are given semi-military training somewhere in Bogor, West Java, presumably by members of the Indonesian military. It is said that members of this group have a strong commitment to the organization and are even willing to die for it.

All FPI members and followers are given Islamic teachings, often by the members of the consultative assembly, who are usually *ulama*. Faith or *aqidah* is one of the most important parts of their training. They are also given the so-called *fiqh al-jihad*, or general Islamic principles concerning *jihad*, including instructions in the motivation, methodology, and practice of *jihad*. The reason for this undertaking is clear—to avoid committing mistakes during the *jihad* that would lessen its impact or prove costly. *Jihad* is understood as a holy duty that has particular requirements in accordance with Islamic teachings.

During Misbahul Anam's tenure as FPI secretary-general from 1998 to 2000, he combined instructions in *fiqh al-jihad* with several litanies and chanting taken from various sources, including the *Tijaniyyah*, a Sufi order in which he was a *murshid* (leader of a mystical association). However, these teachings were discontinued after his resignation in 2000.

The FPI paramilitary organization's hierarchical structure parallels that of the army. It is led by an *imam besar* (great leader). Under him are several *imam*, each of whose authority covers a province. Under an *imam* are several *wali*, whose rule of command covers a region (*kabupaten* or *kotamadya*). The *wali* is also called chief commander (not to be confused with chief leader). Under a *wali* are several *qaid* (commanders), whose jurisdiction covers a *kecamatan* or a district. Under a *qaid* are several *amir*, whose rule of command covers a semi-district. Under an *amir* are several *rais*, whose command extends up to a village. The position of the *rais* is the lowest hierarchical position in the paramilitary organization. All the members of the FPI paramilitary group are under the authority of the department of paramilitary and state defense. Despite the fact that the structure of the FPI is very much like that of the military, Ahmad Shabri Lubis denies this similarity.

The FPI Military Personnel

	Unit/Position	Number of Subordinate Military Personnel
1	*Jundi*	1 person
2	*Rais*	Equivalent to 20 personnel
3	*Amir*	Equivalent to 210 personnel (200 *jundi* + 10 *rais*)
4	*Qaid*	Equivalent to 1,055 personnel (1,000 *jundi* + 5 *amir* + 50 *rais*)
5	*Wali*	Equivalent to 5,280 personnel (5,000 *jundi* + 5 *qaid* + 25 *amir* + 250 *rais*)
6	*Imam*	Equivalent to 26,400 personnel (25,000 *jundi* + 5 *wali* + 25 *qaid* + 125 *amir* + 1,250 *rais*)
7	*Imam Besar*	All the military personnel

Some disciplines practiced by the FPI are said to have been adopted from the Indonesian education system, which in one way or another has adopted military disciplines. During the Suharto era, this discipline became an integrated part of the national education system. Throughout the country students were introduced to the doctrines of patriotism and semi-military disciplines, as can be seen in the obligatory Monday morning events as well as certain national day commemorations where students were mobilized and trained to be loyal to the country. Lubis also denies this comparison, claiming that the FPI military personnel are not equipped with weapons. If there is a weapon, it must be a stick (*toya*) made from bamboo or wood, initially used for a flagstaff, but which, in an emergency situation, can be used as a weapon. He admits that it is difficult for the FPI paramilitary members not to have a weapon. During my visits to the FPI headquarters in the period 1999–2000, however, it was apparent that they were equipped with traditional weapons such as knives and swords.

If we look at the organization's overall structure, at either the national or regional levels, it is obvious that the *majlis syuro* and the executive board are dominated by the members of the *habaib* community. I assume that the presence of the FPI, in one way or another, is a means to accommodate and facilitate the interests of the *habaib*. Their domination can be seen in the fact that nearly all the important positions within the organization are under their control. Since the Jami'at al-Khair (community of righteousness) broke down in the first decades of the twentieth century because of its unending conflict with the Irshadi, an organization dominated by the non-*habaib* Hadhrami, the *habaib* community has had no strong organization that can accommodate its interests. During the Sukarno and Suharto eras, they appear to have been on the periphery of the nation-building processes—in social, religious, and political life. Since the Reformasi, however, many opportunities to control and access public spheres have become available, not only for the *habaib* but also for Muslim people in general. These opportunities have been exploited by the *habaib* as a way of being more involved in public life.

The second component of the organization are young educated Muslims from middle- and low-class families. It is misleading to assume that FPI members consist entirely of uneducated and poor Muslims. Based on my observations, some of its executive board members are young Muslims who have been educated at Middle Eastern universities, several even at secular universities.[94] Most, however, are young Muslims who have studied Islam at various *pesantren* (Islamic boarding schools), *majlis taklim* (centers for religious learning), and mosque-based organizations for young Muslims (*ikatan remaja masjid*). Also significant is that they have relatively diverse religious backgrounds. Many members are attached to the NU and Muhammadiyah, and the remaining do not have religious affiliations.

The organization's third component are uneducated Muslims who have become FPI die-hard loyalists. Most of them are ordinary Muslims who joined the organization because of paranoia. Many are former vigilantes who are committed to return to the path of Allah (*taubat*). Shabri, when criticized because of the presence of numerous former vigilantes within the FPI, argues that the repenting vigilantes are as good as other Muslims who return to the path of God. They are even better than those Muslims who do not have a clear religious stance.

Those who believe that destroying entertainment places represents the very meaning of *jihad* are socially and religiously suspect; they believe that by engaging in these acts, their previous sins will be forgiven by God, and their rewards will be nothing but paradise. Frequently it appears that their senior comrades incite them to take action against certain targets that might have political implications for their seniors' own self-interest. It is said that they are easily mobilized and ready to fight against the enemies of Islam. One of my interviewees said that the FPI can mobilize as many as ten thousand members in just a few hours. During its first anniversary in 1999, it deployed as many as one hundred thousand members and supporters from Jakarta, Tangerang, Bogor, and Bekasi.

The dominance of the *habaib* in the consultative assembly and executive board appears to have led to disintegration and conflict between the *habaib* and non-*habaib*. Both have political interests that are frequently difficult to resolve. Verification of this came in 2000, when Misbahul Anam and Cecep Bustami declared they were leaving the organization. The former was the incumbent secretary-general and one of the founding fathers. He is one of the most outspoken leaders who strongly criticized government policies concerning Muslim affairs. Before joining the organization, he studied in many *pesantren* in Java and grew up in circumstances highly influenced by the NU tradition. He is no longer attached to the NU, however. During his studies at IAIN Syarif Hidayatullah Jakarta in the late 1980s, unlike students with NU backgrounds who usually became activists of the PMII (Indonesian Muslim Students Movement, a students' organization linked to the NU), he joined the modernist Muhammadiyah, although informally. Later, because of his hard-line stance, he joined the PII, the radical Masyumi-linked student organization.

During my interview, Misbahul Anam said that he resigned from the FPI because it had moved away from its original position. According to Anam, the FPI was founded to respond to all the problems of the Muslim people, but later it was involved more frequently in issues that, in his opinion, "have nothing to do with Muslim concerns." While is not quite clear what Anam means by this statement, I assume that the FPI is becoming increasingly dominated by the *habaib* factions, many of whom have been known to be political brokers.[95] Anam's decision to leave the organization has in effect eroded support of his group within the FPI-supported branches around Ciputat, Pamulang, Sawangan, and Depok. Several of my respondents said that they are no longer interested in the FPI since Anam has left: "If Anam leaves, I leave."[96] Afterwards Anam reportedly turned quietist and is only concerned with his *pesantren*.

Meanwhile, Cecep Bustami left the FPI because of his extremely radical standpoint. It appears that the FPI, in many ways, could not accommodate his ideas. Not long after the Kampung Utan meeting, he left the FPI and established the Laskar Hizbullah (Soldiers of the Party of God) in Serang Banten, which has been involved in several actions against entertainment places in Serang. One day his followers were involved in a quarrel with the members of Serang-based *Kopassus* (Special Forces of the Indonesian Military) troops. He was called up by the authorities in Serang to take responsibility for his followers' actions. During one of his trips while in residence at Pandeglang, a group of people, presumably members of the *Kopassus*, stopped his car and shot him dead.

CONCLUDING REMARKS

The emergence of radical Muslim organizations in Indonesia during the last four years can be explained mainly by three interwoven and overlapping factors. The first is that the ideas of fundamentalism are embedded in the body of Islamic teachings. The second factor is related to the state-society relationship. During the Sukarno and Suharto eras, Muslim fundamentalists did not successfully disseminate their ideology because of the leaders' tight political control. But with the advent of the Reformasi era followed by a weak government, political expression was open to everyone. It was during the era of weak government that Islamic fundamentalist organizations emerged and became prominent.

The third factor is that most Muslim people are not prepared to live in what Alvin Toffler calls "the third wave" of modernization and globalization, which has disrupted Muslim life in traditional societies. Fundamentalist Muslims respond to modernization and globalization with suspicion and even rejection.

The FPI appeared as a consequence of the weakened state of Islam following the Reformasi movement in 1998. Its roots are found in the social and religious movements of the 1980s, during which modernization began to pervade the country. Unlike other radical Muslim groups, the FPI has nothing to do with either Darul Islam and Masyumi or transnational Islamic movements. It is simply an expression of Indonesian Muslims' disillusionment with the existing social and political situation.

NOTES

1   There are a number of studies on the emergence of radical Islamicism in Indonesia's post-reformation period. See Chaider S. Bamualim et al., "Radikalisme
Agama dan Perubahan Sosial di DKI Jakarta" (Jakarta: Pusat Bahasa dan Budaya
IAIN Syarif Hidayatullah Jakarta, 1999–2000); Noorhaidi Hasan, "Faith and Politics: The Rise of the Laskar Jihad in the Era of Transition in Indonesia," *Indonesia*,
2002, 145–169; Jajang Jahroni et al., "Agama dan Negara di Indonesia, Studi tentang Pandangan Politik Front Pembela Islam, Laskar Jihad, Ikhwanul Muslimin,
dan Laskar Mujahidin" (Proyek RUKK LIPI, 2002); and Martin van Bruinessen,
Genealogies of Islamic Radicalism in Post-Soeharto Indonesia (ISIM and Utrecht
University, 2003).

2   During Suharto's rule, especially in the 1970s and 1980s, there were no significant Islamic movements because of the government's tight control. However, there
were clandestine movements by Muslim activists. See, for instance, Muhammad
Wildan, "Students and Politics: The Response of the Pelajar Islam Indonesia (PII)
to Politics in Indonesia," master's thesis, Leiden University, 1999; Abdul Syukur,
"Gerakan Usroh di Indonesia, Kasus Peristiwa Lampung," master's thesis, Jakarta,
Fakultas Sastra Universitas Indonesia, 2001.

3   See Faisal Ismail, "Pancasila as the Sole Basis for All Political Parties and for
All Mass Organizations: An Account of Muslims' Responses," *Studia Islamika*
3(4) 1996, 1–92.

4   For studies of Islamic fundamentalism, see Martin E. Marty and R. Scott
Appleby (eds.), *Fundamentalisms Comprehended* (Chicago and London: University of Chicago Press, 1995).

5   Robert W. Hefner, *Civil Islam: Muslims and Democratization in Indonesia*
(Princeton: Princeton University Press, 2000), 58–83.

6   The "Berkeley mafia" refers to the economic architects of the New Order. Its
history goes back to Widjojo Nitisastro, a young economist from the University
of Indonesia (UI), who was asked by Suharto to handle economic problems. Nitisastro created his working team, most of whom were from the UI. During the first
years of the Suharto era, there were many scholarships made available for them
to study economics at the University of California, Berkeley, hence, the coining
of the term, the Berkeley mafia. Not all the members of the Berkeley mafia were
graduates of the University of California, Berkeley, and not all the UI economists
were the members of the Berkeley mafia. It is simply a term to indicate the unseen

but powerful organization that has controlled the economic policies of the last thirty-five years. Its main policy decisions made Indonesia's economy dependent on foreign aid provided by the IMF, World Bank, Paris Club, London Club, IGGI, CGI, etc. Its reminiscences are also seen in the former economic cabinet of Megawati Sukarnoputri. Outspoken Indonesian economists such as Kwik Kian Gie, a critic of the IMF and a former coordinating minister for economy and industry during the first months of Abdurrahman Wahid's presidency, actually believes that the Berkeley mafia still controls the economic policies of Indonesia. See Muh. Indrajit, *Berkeley Mafia dan Ekonomi Indonesia*, http://mail2.factsoft.de/pipermail/national/2002-December/011759.html

7   R. William Liddle, "Indonesia's Unexpected Failure of Leadership" in Adam Schwarz and Jonathan Paris (eds.), *The Politics of Post-Suharto Indonesia* (New York: Council on Foreign Relations Press, 1999), 16–39.

8   Corruption, collusion, and nepotism (Ind. *korupsi, kolusi* and *nepotisme*, abbreviated as KKN) are believed to be the causes of the Indonesian crisis. The reformation movement targets eradicating KKN as well as establishing a good and clean government.

9   Anti-Chinese movements broke out in several places in Indonesia during the New Order era. Raising critical issues concerning the Chinese vs. natives remained a taboo. Matters relating to ethnicity, religion, and race (Ind. SARA) were out of bounds during the New Order era to prevent horizontal conflicts among the Indonesian communities. Chinese people had become the target of violent actions undertaken by certain groups during the outbreak of the Reformasi. It is reported that during those days, thousands of Chinese left the country, heading to Singapore, Malaysia, Australia, and the United States with their capital. During the colonial periods, the Chinese, together with the Arabs, had enjoyed great privilege as they were at the second level (*vreemde oosterlingen*) in the social structure after the Europeans, while the native Indonesians were at the third level.

10   Robert W. Hefner, "Islam and Nation in the Post-Soeharto Era." In Adam Schwarz and Jonathan Paris (eds.), *The Politics of Post-Suharto Indonesia* (New York: Council on Foreign Relations Press, 1999), 49.

11   Olivier Roy, *The Failure of Political Islam* (London: I. B. Tauris, 1994).

12   Robert W. Hefner, *Civil Islam: Muslims and Democratization in Indonesia* (Princeton: Princeton University Press, 2000).

13   Abdurrahman Wahid, the NU traditionalist leader, is one of the Muslim leaders who refused to join the ICMI, arguing that it would only lead to sectarianism.

Meanwhile the modernist Amin Rais, the leader of the Muhammadiyah, joined the ICMI. Later, however, because of his criticism against the pervasive businesses of Suharto's family, he was undermined within the organization.

14 *Harakah, usroh, ikhwan,* and *akhwat* are terms used by the Muslim Brotherhood-based organization. However, to my understanding, they are consistent with Shiite thought.

15 Muhammad Said Damanik, *Fenomena Partai Keadilan* (Jakarta: Risalah Gusti, 2002).

16 Jalaluddin Rakhmat, one of the young Muslim intellectuals involved in the campus Islamization movements, wrote a book that shows the spirit behind the search for a new model of Islam, *Islam Alternatif* (Bandung: Mizan, 1986).

17 For the Muslim Brotherhood, the interpretation of *shahada* begins with *ilah*, meaning that all ideological, emotional, and material concepts are beyond Allah. Based on this understanding, they proceed to investigate the sources of secular ideologies like Pancasila, capitalism, socialism, etc. Given this indoctrination, the *ikhwan* and the *akhwat* are strongly opposed to Pancasila and its secular dimensions.

18 In the post-Iranian revolution, there emerged a number of Shiite propaganda efforts made by the Iranian embassy in Jakarta. The pictures of Ayatollah Ruhollah Khomeini, Allamah Murtadha Muthahhari, and Allamah Taba Tabai were hung in mosques, schools, offices, and houses. Many Muslim activists idolized them as the modern heroes of Islam. Books, leaflets, and pamphlets on Iran and Shiism were handed out freely to students and Muslim organizations. This propaganda made Saudi Arabia and the rich gulf countries worried about the impact of the revolution. As a result they provided many donations to *madrasah*, mosques, and *pesantren*, and provided scholarships for study in Saudi Arabia.

19 Based on my observations, the Muslim Brotherhood did not establish its network until the beginning of the 1970s, when a young Muslim activist named Hilmi Aminuddin, an al-Azhar graduate, had a great following among the Indonesian Muslim activists. He moved from one place to another to avoid the authorities. Even among the members of the Muslim Brotherhood themselves, he was unknown, and he communicated only with the inner circles.

20 Manuel Castells, *The Power of Identity* (Malden, Mass.: Blackwell Publishers, 1997), 18.

21 Ibid., 18–19.

22 The term Hadhrami refers to the community of people who migrated to Southeast Asia from Hadhramaut, an ancient region in the southern part of the Republic of Yemen. The history of the Hadhrami community in Indonesia goes back to the eighteenth and nineteenth centuries, when a large group of Hadhrami left their country looking for a better life. The Hadhrami are divided into two groups based on their genealogical relationship with the Prophet Muhammad: the Sayyids and the non-Sayyids. The Sayyids are those who claim to be the direct descendants of the Prophet. There has been a long-standing conflict between the Sayyids and non-Sayyids on the claims of who is the real Sayyid. The former established an organization, Jami'at al-Khair, exclusively belonging to them, while the latter established al-Ishlah wa'l Irshad. See Natalie Mobini-Kesheh, *The Hadrami Awakening, Community and Identity in the Netherlands East Indies*, 1900–1942 (Ithaca: Cornell University Press, 1999).

23 On Sayyid Uthman ibn Abdullah ibn Yahya, see Azyumardi Azra, "Hadhrami Scholars in the Malay-Indonesian Diaspora: A Preliminary Study of Sayyid Uthman," *Studia Islamika* 2(2) 1995: 1–33.

24 Badru Salam, "Kepemimpinan Dakwah Al Habib Muhammad Rizieq Bin Husein Syihab," Skripsi, (Fakultas Dakwah, UIN Syarif Hidayatullah Jakarta, 2002).

25 Natalie Mobinie-Kesheh, *The Hadrami Awakening*, 71–90.

26 Natalie Mobinie-Kesheh, *The Hadrami Awakening*.

27 Azyumardi Azra, "Hadhrami Scholars," 1–33.

28 Natalie Mobinie-Kesheh, *The Hadrami Awakening*.

29 Ahl al-Sunnah wal Jama'ah is a theological school, rooted in the tradition of the Companions and the Prophet Muhammad. Abu Hasan al-Ashari is the forerunner of this theology as he developed Ash'arism, an attempt to bridge the gap between the extreme Mu'tazilism, which teaches the superiority of reason over revelation, and the Jabbarism, which teaches human predestination.

30 Tanah Abang is one of the most important Hadhrami settlements in Jakarta. Its history goes back to the beginning of the nineteenth century, when a large number of the Hadhrami migrated to that area and developed it as a religious and business center. Nowadays Tanah Abang has become one of the most densely populated slum areas in Jakarta. Since it was developed as a center for the garment industry in the beginning of the 1970s, a number of ethnic groups have gone there looking for a better life. Pasar Tanah Abang, the most important business center in that area, is allegedly controlled by vigilantes who are backed by military personnel.

It is a perfect picture of Indonesia's contradictions, where *madrasah* and mosque are located side by side with prostitution, crime, vigilantism, and poverty.

31 *Kemungkaran* is a term to indicate all sinful deeds such as adultery, gambling, alcoholism, crime, corruption, etc., which are forbidden by Islam. *Kemaksiatan* or *maksiat* (Arabic: *ma'shyia*) has the same meaning as that of *kemungkaran*.

32 During the 1980s, the government exerted tight control over Muslim preachers. All the preachers were licensed by the government through the Kopkamtib (Command for Operation, Security and Order) led by (Marine) General Sudomo.

33 *Ustadz, ulama,* and *kyai* are titles given to those involved in teaching the Islamic religion. Most of them usually preach and are therefore called preacher (Ind. *penceramah*). Instead of using such titles, the Hadhrami use *sayyid* as an honorific title. The use of *habib* as honorific title did not begin until the late 1960s.

34 I saw pictures of high-ranking military officials in Misbahul Anam's house. Many of my respondents say that a number of men in military uniforms went to his house frequently prior to the emergence of the FPI and during its first years. They say that national intelligence agencies have used their information.

35 Adi Sasono, "Kita Masuk Skenario Orang Lain," http://www.hamline.edu/apakabar/basisdata/1998/12/09/0012.html

36 Olivier Roy, *The Failure of Political Islam* (London: I. B. Tauris, 1994), 9.

37 General Wiranto is believed to be part of the the "red and white military faction." The "green military faction" includes General Prabowo, the son-in-law of former president Suharto, who, prior to the reformation, approached a number of Muslim leaders, including Din Syamsuddin. See Robert W. Hefner, *Civil Islam: Muslims and Democratization in Indonesia* (Princeton: Princeton University Press, 2000).

38 Wiranto was one the Indonesian military officers charged by the media and Western countries of committing human rights violations in the post-East Timor referendum.

39 My research informant says that the military interest in the FPI is because it can be used to counterattack the Forkot (Forum of the City), an extreme left-wing student organization, presumably supported by secular and Christian groups, that criticized the military because of their close relationship with Muslim groups. This assumption is paralleled by the presence of Muslim student movements such as Hammas (Muslim Students Intra-Campus Association) and KAMMI (United Action of Indonesian Muslim Students), which were founded to balance the maneuvers made by the Forkot and Christian student movements.

40 Habibie was disqualified because he was considered one of Suharto's cronies. He was known as Suharto's golden boy, enjoying great privileges during Suharto's presidency. One of his controversial projects was the Indonesian aircraft manufacturing project, which required a huge amount of money. To build this, he used the money initially allocated for a forestry greening project.

41 During the Special Session of the People's Consultative Assembly, the military reportedly recruited as many as one hundred thousand paramilitary groups. See Martin van Bruinessen, *Genealogies of Islamic Radicalism in Post-Soeharto Indonesia*.

42 Interview with Ahmad Shabri Lubis, FPI secretary-general.

43 Jakarta has become the PPP's political stronghold since the beginning of the New Order era. It is also strong in some parts of West Java, Central Java, Sumatra, and Kalimantan. Hamzah's approaches to certain radical Islamic groups have surprised many people. He attended the Laskar Jihad's national congress in Jakarta in 2002. This visit was controversial since its top leader, Ja'far Umar Thalib, was in police detention.

44 On the Laskar Jihad, see Chaider S. Bamualim et al., *Radikalisme Agama dan Perubahan Sosial di DKI Jakarta*; Noorhaidi Hasan, "Faith and Politics: The Rise of the Laskar Jihad in the Era of Transition in Indonesia"; Jajang Jahroni et al., "Agama dan Negara di Indonesia." On the roles of the Laskar Jihad in Ambon, see Mohammad Shoelhi, Laskar Jihad, Kambing Hitam Konflik Maluku (Jakarta: Pustaka Zaman, 2002).

45 On Abu Bakar Ba'asyir, see Idi Subandy Ibrahim and Asep Syamsul M. Romli, *Kontroversi Ba'syir, Jihad Melawan Opini "Fitnah" Global* (Bandung: Yayasan Nuansa Cendikia, 2003).

46 Jajang Jahroni et al., "Agama dan Negara di Indonesia." See also "Ada Pembunuhan Diam Saja, Itu Politik," Interview with Munir http://aliansi.hypermart.net/1999/10/topik4.html

47 See Hermawan Sulistyo, *Palu Arit di Ladang Tebu, Sejarah Pembantaian Massal Yang Terlupakan* (Jakarta: Gramedia, 2000).

48 Based on this act, communism with its all manifestations is stated to be a banned ideology in Indonesia.

49 According to the survey made by the PPIM, communists are the group most despised by Muslims, followed by Jews, Chinese, Christians, and the radical Islamic groups.

50 Tanjung Priok is a district in the northern part of Jakarta. A number of ethnic groups such as Buginese, Makassarese, Javanese, and Betawenese live there. The incident started with a group of police officers, who warned Muslim people in that area to take down all posters hung in a local mosque urging people to refuse Pancasila as the sole basis for social and political life. The following day, the police returned to the mosque and found the pamphlets were still there. They immediately entered the mosque without taking their shoes off and pulled down the pamphlets. This angered the congregation and led to the burning of the police motorcycles. As a result, a number of people were sentenced. The following day, people gathered in the mosque in an attempt to release their friends. Amir Biki, the dissident leader who became the victim, led them to attack the police station. On route, they were intercepted by a unit of military troops. Some negotiations were made to persuade them to return to their houses, but they refused. The situation suddenly became uncontrollable ending in a massacre. According to one version, a hundred Muslims were killed during the incident, and many others were sentenced. During the Reformasi period, this case emerged again into public debate after a gap of fifteen years. The KOMNASHAM (National Commission for Human Rights), in its report, concluded that only a dozen had been killed by *force majeur*. Many of the Islamic organizations, including the FPI, rejected this report and attacked its office in Menteng, Jakarta.

51 Habib Muhammad Rizieq Syihab, "Kita Justru Akan Semakin Keras," *Adil* 3(7) 18–24 December 2000.

52 The FPI's opposition against Wahid is actually unclear. When a number of Muslim organizations asked Wahid to step down, the FPI remained calm. Rizieq says diplomatically that if that process fits the national constitution, he will support it. In an invitation made by Wahid, Rizieq said that he actually despised those people who criticized Wahid personally, saying that Wahid was also one of his teachers and he himself was in fact a member of the NU.

53 A number of radical Islamic groups relate Syafei's speech to the Kupang and Ambon incidents. They believe that the speech instigated conflicts in both areas. However, the case remains deadlocked. Meanwhile moderate Muslim leaders such as Abdurrahman Wahid and Nurcholish Madjid give a considerably different opinion. The former believes that such a case is only slander, while the latter says that it is an "incident." A solution is for Syafei to explain the truth to the Muslim people and apologize if necessary. Since his resignation from the military, Syafei was active in the PDIP (Indonesian Struggle Democratic Party) led by President

Megawati Soekarnoputri, and seems to be among the elites who control the party.

54 Jajang Jahroni et al., "Agama dan Negara di Indonesia."

55 Interview with Zainuddin, the FPI paramilitary coordinator.

56 Interview with Ustadz Ja'far Shiddiq, the LJ coordinator.

57 I am not certain whether the FPI has actually made sweeping actions against expatriates. Official police information indicated that sweeping rarely occurs in Jakarta. In some cities, I have heard that some radical Islamic groups have actually made sweepings. The FPI's threats of sweeping have caused anxiety among expatriates. See "Religious Groups Threaten to Expel Americans from Indonesia." http://198.65.147.194/English/News/2001-09/22/article9.shtml; Lindsay Murdoch, "Islamic threat to hit Americans," http://old.smh.com.au/news/0109/20/world/world15.html.

58 Interview with Ahmad Shabri Lubis.

59 Ibid.

60 Interview with Misbahul Anam.

61 As many as 98 percent of the FPI paramilitary troops are repenting vigilantes. Interview with Zainuddin, FPI coordinator.

62 The media has played an important role in creating a frightening image of the FPI. There are many social and *dakwah* activities which have never been covered by the media.

63 "Ye are the best people, evolved for mankind, enjoining what is right, forbidding what is wrong, and believing in God. If only the People of the Book had faith, it were best for them: among them are some who have faith, but most of them are perverted transgressors." (Qur'an 3: 110). In one of the Prophet's sayings, it is said. "Whosoever sees corruption among ye, he/she should change it with his/her hand. If he/she can't do that, he/she should change it with his/her words. If he/she can't do that, he/she should change it with his/her heart. And that is the weakest faith."

64 Habib Muhammad Rizieq Syihab, "Kita Justru Akan Semakin Keras," *Tekad* 3(7): 18–24 December 2000.

65 Jajang Jahroni et al., "Agama dan Negara di Indonesia."

66 "Operasi Jeda Maksiat ala FPI," http://www.detik.com/peristiwa/2000/12/01/2000121-040837.shtml.

67 "Invite (all) to the way of thy Lord with wisdom and beautiful preaching and argue with them in ways that are best and most gracious, for thy Lord knoweth best who have strayed from His Path, and who receive guidance" (Qur'an 16: 125).

68 Interview with Ahmad Shabri Lubis, FPI secretary-general.

69 The word *ganyang* had been used by the PKI (Indonesian Communist Party) members as a slogan to fight their enemies. It is unlikely a coincidence that the FPI uses this word to wake up the spirit of resistance among the oppressed people to fight against the establishment as the PKI did before.

70 "Operasi Jeda Maksiat ala FPI," http://www.detik.com/peristiwa/2000/12/01/2000121-040837.shtml.

71 Depok is a new settlement located in the southern part of Jakarta. It was developed during the late 1970s as a result of urbanization. Many Muslims moved to this area and built mosques, *pesantren*, and other Islamic schools. Sawangan is known as the stronghold of the Nahdatul Ulama and Muhammadiyah. Meanwhile Parung is a relatively new area developed after the Jakarta-Bogor highway was built in the 1980s. This green area attracts financiers to invest in amusement businesses. Parung has been known as the place where many "dimming places" (*warung remang-remang*) for hidden prostitution are found.

72 The ideology of the FPI can be found in Habib Muhammad Rizieq Syihab, *Dialog Piagam Jakarta* (Jakarta: Pustaka Sidah, 2000).

73 Jajang Jahroni, "Islamic Fundamentalism in Contemporary Indonesia," *Refleksi* 4(1) 2002.

74 In 2001, the percentage of those who agreed with the application of Islamic law was 61.4. In 2002, this percentage increased to 71 percent. This survey has been misunderstood by a number of radical Islamic groups as evidence of the growing aspiration among Muslims for the application of Islamic law. See "Barometer Indonesia untuk Konsolidasi Demokrasi" (Jakarta: PPIM, 2002). See *Tempo*, December 29, 2002.

75 See *Gerakan Pembangunan Masyarakat Berakhlaqul Karima*. http://www.cianjur.go.id/marhamah/htm.

76 Interview with Ahmad Shabri Lubis.

77 Ibid.

78 Habib Muhammad Rizieq Syihab, *Dialog Piagam Jakarta* (Jakarta: Pustaka Sidah, 2000).

79 Allegiance to the Republic of Indonesia can be found in the following decree concerning women's appointment as president following the election of Megawati Sukarnoputri, the incumbent vice president, after Abdurrahman Wahid's impeachment in 2000. "The Oath of FPI Paramilitary Members. We, the members of the FPI paramilitary, fully support the Decree of the Islamic Defenders Front on woman's appointment as a president. We promise to the state: (1) to guard the unity of the State of the Republic of Indonesia, (2) to guard the unity of the Indonesian nation, (3) to guard the security, order, and safety of the Republic of Indonesia, (4) to obey all the government's policies as long as they are in accordance with the Constitution and not against the Islamic teachings, (5) to become the guardians of the Republic of Indonesia believing in and fearing Allah the Almighty." The Decree of the FPI on Woman's Appointment as president (Jakarta: The FPI Secretary, July 24, 2001).

80 Interview with Ahmad Shabri Lubis, the Secretary General of the FPI.

81 Martin van Bruinessen, *Genealogies of Islamic Radicalism in post-Suharto Indonesia.*

82 There are hundreds of NGOs that focus on drug abuse in the country. This phenomenon is an expression of how concerned people are about drug abuse. These movements have been supported by all members of the community including Muslim organizations, celebrities, women, and students' organizations.

83 A. A. Maramis (a Christian) is the only non-Muslim member of the Commission of Nine.

84 Pancasila consists of five principles: (1). *Ketuhanan Yang Maha Esa* (Belief in One God); (2) *Kemanusiaan Yang Adil dan Beradab* (Humanity based on justice and civility); (3) *Persatuan Indonesia* (The unity of Indonesia); (4) *Kerakyatan Yang Dipimpin oleh Hikmat Permusyawaratan/Perwakilan*. People are led by wisdom in the consultative and representative form; (5) *Keadilan bagi Seluruh Rakyat Indonesia* (Social justice for all Indonesian citizens).

85 For debate on the Jakarta Charter, see H. Endang Saifuddin Anshari, *Piagam Jakarta 22 Juni 1945 dan Sejarah Konsensus Nasional antara Nasionalis Islami dan Nasionalis 'Sekuler' tentang Dasar Negara Republik Indonesia, 1945–1959* (Bandung: Pustaka, 1981).

86 For debate on Islam as state ideology during the parliamentary era, see Ahmad Syafi'i Ma'arif, "Islam as the Basis of State: A Study of the Islamic Political Ideas as Reflected in the Constituent Assembly Debates in Indonesia," PhD dissertation, University of Chicago, 1983.

87 Habib Muhammad Rizieq Syihab, *Dialog Piagam Jakarta* (Jakarta: Pustaka Ibnu Sidah, 2000).

88 Nahdatul Ulama and Muhammadiya reject the idea of reinstating the Jakarta Charter. A number of Muslim intellectuals such as Abdurrahman Wahid, Nurcholish Madjid, A. Syafi'i Ma'arif, Masdar F. Mas'udi, and Ulil Abshar Abdalla reject the Jakarta Charter as well as the amendment of Article 29 of the Constitution.

89 See Nurcholish Madjid, "Kotak 'Pandora' Bernama UUD '45" http://www.kjri-hkg.org.hk/penerangan/nasional-16.htm.

90 Ahmad Shabri Lubis is the third secretary-general of the FPI. The first was K.H. Misbahul Anam and the second was Muhammad Reza Pahlevi, S.Ag.

91 The FPI Surakarta is one of the most active Muslim organizations in the country. It appears that it has been influenced much more by the MMI (Majelis Mujahidin Indonesia, Forum of the Indonesian Fighters), the Abu Bakar Ba'asyir-led Islamic organization, which in many ways interprets Islam differently from the FPI.

92 Martin van Bruinessen, *Genealogies of Islamic Radicalism in Post-Suharto Indonesia.*

93 Quote by Habib Muhammad Rizieq Syihab. In Jajang Jahroni, et al., "Agama dan Negara di Indonesia."

94 As many as 20 percent of the FPI paramilitary members are university graduates. The total number of FPI paramilitary members in Jakarta in 2000 was 5200. Interview with Ustadz Zainuddin.

95 During Abdurrahman Wahid's presidency he accused a *habib* named Ali Ba'aqil, a member of the FPI *majlis syuro*, of helping Tomi Suharto.

96 Syu'iab Sumaryadi, the FPI supporter from Ciputat.

BIBLIOGRAPHY

Aglionby, John. "The Secret Role of the Army in Sowing the Seeds of Religious Strife." *The Guardian*, October 16, 2002.

Al-Chaidar. *Sepak Terjang KW 9 Abu Toto Syekh A. S. Panji Gumilang Menyeleweng-kan NKA-NII Pasca S. M. Kartosuwirjo*. Jakarta: Madani Press, 2000.

Anshari, H. Endang Saifuddin. *Piagam Jakarta 22 Juni 1945 dan Sejarah Konsensus Nasional antara Nasionalis Islami dan Nasionalis 'Sekuler' tentang Dasar Negara Republik Indonesia, 1945–1959*. Bandung: Pustaka, 1981.

Azra, Azyumardi. "Hadhrami Scholars in the Malay-Indonesian Diaspore: a Preliminary Study of Sayyid Uthman." *Studia Islamika* 2(2) (1995): 1–33.

Badan Litbang Departemen Agama dan Diklat Keagamaan (Research and Development Institution of the Department of Religious Afffairs). "Kajian Gerakan Islam Kontemporer Era Reformasi." November 20, 2002.

Bamualim, Chaider S. et al. "Radikalisme Agama dan Perubahan Sosial di DKI Jakarta." Jakarta: Pusat Bahasa dan Budaya IAIN Syarif Hidayatullah Jakarta, 1999–2000.

Bolland, B. J. *The Struggle of Islam in Modern Indonesia*. The Hague: Martinus Nijhoff, 1971.

Bruinnessen, Martin van. *Genealogies of Islamic Radicalism in Post-Soeharto Indonesia*. ISIM and Utrecht University, 2003.

Burke, Edmund, and Ira M. Lapidus (eds.). *Islam, Politics, and Social Movements*. Los Angeles: University of California Press, 1988.

Castells, Manuel. *The Power of Identity*. Malden, Mass.: Blackwell Publishers, 1997.

Chew, Amy. "Indonesian Radicals Call for Blood." *CNN*, March 20, 2003.

Damanik, Muhammad Said. *Fenomena Partai Keadilan*. Jakarta: Risalah Gusti, 2002.

"The Decree of the FPI on Woman's Appointment as President." Jakarta: The FPI Secretary, July 24, 2001.

Dijk, C. van. *Rebellion under the Banner of Islam: the Darul Islam in Indonesia*. The Hague: Martinus Nijhoff, 1981.

Eickelman, Dale F. and James Piscatori. *Muslim Politics*. Princeton: Princeton University Press, 1996.

Enayat, Hamid. *Modern Islamic Political Thought*. Austin: University of Texas Press, 1982.

Firestone, Reuven. *Jihad, the Origin of Holy War in Islam*. New York: Oxford University Press, 1999.

Guerin, Bill. "The Simmering Threat of Indonesian Radicalism." *Asia Time*, September 12, 2002.

Hasan, Noorhaidi. "Faith and Politics: The Rise of the Laskar Jihad in the Era of Transition in Indonesia." *Indonesia*: 2(4) (2002): 145–169.

Hathout, Hassan. *Reading the Muslim Mind*. Burr Ridge, Ill.: American Trust Publications, 2002.

Hefner, Robert W. *Civil Islam: Muslims and Democratization in Indonesia*. Princeton: Princeton University Press, 2000.

Ibrahim, Idi Subandy, Asep Syamsul, and M. Romli. *Kontroversi Ba'syir, Jihad Melawan Opini "Fitnah" Global*. Bandung: Yayasan Nuansa Cendikia, 2003.

Ismail, Faisal. "Pancasila as the Sole Basis for All Political Parties and for All Mass Organizations: An Account of Muslims' Responses." *Studia Islamika* 3(4) 1996, 1–92.

Jahroni, Jajang. "Islamic Fundamentalism in Contemporary Indonesia." *Refleksi* 4(1) (2002).

_____ et al. "Agama dan Negara di Indonesia, Studi tentang Pandangan Politik Front Pembela Islam, Laskar Jihad, Ikhwanul Muslimin, dan Laskar Mujahidin." Proyek RUKK LIPI (unpublished article), 2002.

Kompas. "FPI: Goyang Ngebor Maksiat!" May 2, 2003. In Indonesian.

Ma'arif, Syafi'i. "Islam as the Basis of State: A Study of the Islamic Political Ideas as Reflected in the Constituent Assembly Debates in Indonesia." PhD dissertation, University of Chicago, 1983

Marty, Martin E., and R. Scott Appleby (eds.). *Fundamentalisms Comprehended*. Chicago and London: University of Chicago Press, 1995.

Mobini-Kesheh, Natalie. *The Hadrami Awakening: Community and Identity in the Netherlands East Indies, 1900–1942*. Ithaca: Cornell University Press, 2000.

Muhammad Rizieq Syihab, Habib. *Dialog Piagam Jakarta*. Jakarta: Pustaka Sidah, 2000.

_____. *Dialog Amar Ma'ruf Nahyi Munkar: Menjawab Berbagai Tuduhan Terhadap Gerakan Amar Ma'ruf Nahyi Munkar di Indonesia.* Jakarta: Pustaka Sidah, forthcoming.

Noer, Deliar. *Gerakan Moderen Islam di Indonesia 1900–1942.* Jakarta: LP3ES, 1996.

Purnomo, Alip. FPI *Disalahpahami.* Jakarta: Mediatama Indonesia, 2003.

Panjimas. "Kita Masuk Skenario Orang Lain." December 9, 1998.

Pikiran Rakyat. "Ba'asyir Dituduh Dirikan NII." April 24, 2003. In Indonesian.

_____. "Desak MPR Masukkan dalam Konstitusi, Ormas Islam Tuntut Syariah Bisa Diberlakukan." August 6, 2002. In Indonesian.

Rakhmat, Jalaluddin. *Islam Alternatif.* Bandung: Mizan, 1986.

Roy, Olivier. *The Failure of Political Islam.* London: I. B. Tauris, 1994.

Salam, Badru. *Kepemimpinan Dakwah Al Habib Muhammad Rizieq Bin Husein Shihab, Skripsi.* Fakultas Dakwah, UIN Syarif Hidayatullah Jakarta, 2002.

Schwarz, Adam, and Jonathan Paaris (eds.). *The Politics of Post-Suharto Indonesia.* New York: Council on Foreign Relations Press, 1999.

Shoelhi, Mohammad. *Laskar Jihad, Kambing Hitam Konflik Maluku.* Jakarta: Pustaka Zaman, 2002.

Suara Merdeka. "Menang Kawal Demo Ormas Islam." August 6, 2002.

Sulistyo, Hermawan. *Palu Arit di Ladang Tebu, Sejarah Pembantaian Massal Yang Terlupakan.* Jakarta: Gramedia, 2000.

Suminta, H. Aqib. *Politik Islam Hindia Belanda.* Jakarta: LP3ES, 1985.

Syukur, Abdul. "Gerakan Usroh di Indonesia, Kasus Peristiwa Lampung." Master's thesis, Jakarta: Fakultas Sastra Universitas Indonesia, 2001.

Taher, Tarmizi, et al. *Radikalisme Agama*, Bahtiar Effendi and Hendro Prasetyo (eds.). Jakarta: PPIM-IAIN Jakarta, 1998.

Wildan, Muhammad. "Students and Politics: The Response of the Pelajar Islam Indonesia (II) to Politics in Indonesia." Master's thesis, Leiden University, 1999.

Yunanto, S. et al. *Militant Islamic Movement in Indonesia and South East Asia.* Jakarta: Friedrich-Ebert-Stiftung and the Ridep Institute, n.d.

ISLAM IN SOUTHEAST ASIA: VIEWS FROM WITHIN
Research Fellowship Program for Young Muslim Scholars

The fellowship program aims to enhance understanding of Islam in Southeast Asia from an "insider's perspective" while building the research capacity of young Muslim scholars and offering them publishing opportunities. Small grants are awarded annually for innovative research on issues concerning socio-political and cultural changes taking place in the diverse Muslim communities of Southeast Asia, especially as they relate to modernization and globalization. Key themes include: popular manifestations of Islam; shaping of Muslim identities in Southeast Asia by regional and globalizing forces; changing gender dynamics in Muslim communities; and the way Islamic values inform economic activities and social responsibilities.

Initiated in 2002, the program is managed by the secretariat of the Asian Muslim Action Network (AMAN) in Bangkok, Thailand, with the advice of leading experts from the region and the financial support of the Rockefeller Foundation.

Information on the program and how to apply can be found at
http://fellowship.arf-asia.org/

AMAN/ARF
House 1562/113, Soi 1/1
Mooban Pibul, Pracharaj Road
Bangkok 10800, Thailand

Tel: 66-2-9130196 • Fax: 66-2-9130197

E-mail: aman@arf-asia.org
http://www.arf-asia.org/aman